Help!
I've just given birth
to a
Teen-ager

PAT BAKER

BAKER BOOK HOUSE
Grand Rapids, Michigan 49506

ISBN: 0-8010-0799-2

Fifth printing, November 1984

Printed in the United States of America

Acknowledgments

In love and gratitude, I thank:

my daughter, Beth, for that special day when she, unknowingly, gave me the idea for this book;

my other two daughters, Dana and Pamela, for giving me the "go ahead" to share stories of their teen-age years;

my husband, Don, who often ate his sandwiches alone while I wrote in seclusion;

my young friend, Linda Smith Tappmeyer, who showed me no mercy as she proofread my manuscript, but at the same time continued to believe in what I was doing;

all those parents who took time out from their busy lives to share with me what they were experiencing with their teens;

and that special group of teen-agers who gave me straightforward answers to questions I asked them during interviews—they reaffirmed the endless love I knew I would always have for them.

Contents

Preface
Help Is on the Way

I am not a family therapist, a child psychologist, or a professional counselor. There are no framed credentials hanging above my kitchen sink, over the washing machine, or on the ironing board. I am a mother of teen-agers, a position I have held for many years.

I have struggled during these years, many times in ignorance, as I tried to awaken my senses to better understand the complex situations that each of our teens was facing. Often I wondered if I would be able to guide them through these experiences. I found myself calling for help, as other parents of teen-agers have called for help, and I felt that no one was hearing me. Now I hope to answer some of those calls.

This book takes a personal approach. I have not put together a list of statistics or done extensive scientific research, but I can talk about things that go on behind the doors of homes. This is where parents, not professionals, have access. I hope these insights will help you begin to understand how other parents have handled these years with their teens.

I couldn't have written about those "awful" years until now. I was much too close to my subjects, too close to their boyfriend problems, late hours, and endless activities. I couldn't talk about those things, much less write about them. I would have been frightened and probably would have frightened you if I had shared many of the struggles I was experiencing. I loved my daughters during those years, but many times I couldn't understand what was going on in their lives. I needed help, for my built-in parental intuition was not sufficient.

In 1968 I made a significant entry in my daily journal. Our oldest daughter was fourteen years old and our second daughter was fast approaching the teen-age years. I was hurting with each word as I wrote:

> I can't understand the world of our teen-ager. I have always had the idea that being a mother always meant being loved, needed and wanted. My relationship with my daughter is not good at this time. I need help! I feel like a failure! I hope these feelings will go away. Don't kids know that parents have feelings, too? I feel so frustrated and inadequate. I'm tired but I can't sleep.

Ten years later, as I reread this entry and considered the situation that had caused me to write it, I was able to look at it objectively for the first time. I began to understand that our daughter was using her natural mechanisms to develop independence from her parents; I was mistaking this as a period of personal defiance toward me.

After that entry, I kept recording how I felt. I continued groping my way through difficult times with the girls, hurting with them, identifying with them. Sometimes I felt like one large, exposed nerve, and at those times all my attempts at wonderful motherhood failed.

I realize now that I was trying to make growing up easy for them. I wanted them to be happy all the time. I didn't want them to feel awkward, make mistakes, or be hurt by others. What foolish goals these were! I was actually unwilling to "let go" and allow them to experience the realities of life, or make some of the same mistakes I had made at that age.

Many of my journal entries in those days expressed frustration. However, it became evident as I read further that intermingled with the negative feelings was a growing satisfaction. As I watched those teens, I saw them emerge as stable, beautiful human beings who were showing signs of mustering courage to enter an adult world. I came to realize that sometimes the hardest days of parenting could later result in days of great joy. This is why I want to share with you the many things I've learned—not to keep you from inevitable tangles with your teens, but to cushion your feelings of frustration, inadequacy, and hopelessness.

I believe in teen-agers. I admire their determination and their frankness. I love how they disguise their tenderness, how they are naturals at finding simple solutions to big problems, how they tolerate adults. I realize that those who won't smile back at me are hurting so deeply that they can't smile.

Teens are human. They hurt, they get confused, they cry. Yet some adults talk about them as though they are not living, breathing beings. I suppose this is because these adults concentrate on a minority of teens who have chosen to withdraw from or rebel against society. They read the bizarre stories of teens and the drug scene, the teen suicides, the runaways, the unwed-mother statistics. But there is a large group of teens who don't get mentioned in the news media at all. The majority are not deeply disturbed, are not resistant to parental values. Full of goals, compassion, and spirit, they stay at home, learning to live with demanding adults and bothersome brothers and sisters.

That's why I bristle when people start making generalizations about teen-agers. It's as ridiculous as assuming that all teens will be six feet tall, or will all play in the high-school band, or will all be good in sports, or will all be cheerleaders, or will all resist parental control and will all be rebellious. Generalizations do not bring about understanding.

So what does? It looks easy on paper, but understanding comes simply by observing, listening, participating, and caring. Read about teen-agers, take time with your own, and *try* to keep up with them. To balance any mistakes along the way, make sure you continue to show a genuine love for who they are. And remember, you must be willing not to expect a generous amount of love in return—at least, not for a while.

Teens are pleading to be understood, and understanding is necessary to keep the teen years from being years of constant power struggles. You are the one who sees them at their worst. They keep their masks on in public, but at home the masks come off and you see the real people. You can see how they've been hurt, or disappointed, and how tired they are from dealing with peer and adult pressures.

While you are in the process of understanding your teens, put your instincts to work. Let your convictions guide you, sleep revitalize you, and prayer sustain you. If you don't have a sense of humor you'd better develop one—or borrow one—before you get too far into those teen years. Some situations have a way of getting so complicated that laughter is the only way to provide relief.

Someone asked me several years ago, "How do you get through the teen years?" I half-jokingly answered, "You pray a lot!" But the more I thought about my answer, the more I realized how accurate it was. Each of our children's lives has been overshadowed with prayer. This gave me a reserve of spiritual wisdom, patience, and understanding that could be dipped into at various times of the day for unexpected occasions.

I would not be completely honest with you if I told you that my husband and I have reared our children alone. I believe that there is a supreme purpose for the birth of every child, and therefore supreme guidance is needed. I will not be saying many things about God's guidance in the contents of this book, but I hope you will be able to detect the overtones of His direction as I write.

In each chapter of this book, I have inserted what I call "Time Outs." Most of them are simple, workable activities that can be done in any family. They require little preparation and can be modified to fit your family's specific needs.

If you can see the value in a particular Time Out, and you feel that it can help correct a weak spot in your relationships with your teens, encourage everyone's participation. There will be times when you will want to explain *why* you're presenting certain Time Outs to your family. On other occasions, you will simply want to begin them naturally, in casual, unplanned settings. If there is opposition to participation in these Time Outs, ask your teens how they would like to go about strengthening those particular family-problem areas.

One Time Out that I didn't include but that should be used in every home is for each family member to communicate "I love you" in some way to every other member no less than once a day. It's amazing what this phrase, unexpected, unannounced, unrehearsed, can do to the atmosphere of a home.

Pat Baker

The Birth

Many expectant parents attend childbirth classes. They see films of the birth process. They are given tours of hospital labor and delivery rooms. They hear lectures about how to bathe, feed, and diaper their new baby. After their child is born, parents can choose from a myriad of baby books which discuss transitions that will occur from babyhood to childhood—the first two phases.

But the teen birth does not take place over a nine-month waiting period. No one has ever been able to explain in three easy steps how parents can fully prepare themselves for the birth of their teen-agers.

According to the baby books, at six months of age, babies are able to sit alone. At age one, they begin to make attempts at walking. These books tell new parents what can be expected of their children at each age level throughout infancy and childhood. But it is difficult to know exactly when the teen years will begin and when they will end. Parents can, of course, look for signs of growing up and out of childhood. When parents begin to understand the progressions from birth to childhood to teen-age years, they can more readily accept the changes that come with each phase.

Changes Parents Notice

You face new patterns of change with your teens. Life is more complex. Instead of your child hiding small, decayed teeth under a pillow at the rate of twenty-five cents per tooth, your teen-ager now has a mouthful of braces —and you make monthly payments to an orthodontist. You won't be able to recall the last kiss you received from your teens in public. You may not even remember the last kiss you got from them.

You are also noticing changes taking place at the meal table. There is less milk spilled. No one is counting to see who got the most cherries from the fruit cocktail or who got the largest serving of meat or dessert. And you, the parent, will now occasionally get to taste the savory parts of the chicken breast or thigh, instead of the wings and back.

In the past, table conversations followed this general progression: "Mom, he's looking at me." "Dad, he's crunching in my ear." "She got the piece I wanted." "He got all the sugar at the bottom of the cereal box." "Hey! who's got their feet on my side?" These comments are being replaced by locker-room jokes, talk of who's dating whom, or gossip about teachers. When it's time to do the dishes, these teens are ingenious at remembering that they have to study for a big test, practice their piano, voice, or cheers, lift weights or jog.

The girls begin showing interest in boys instead of Barbie and Ken dolls. Movies take the place of comic books. Story books are replaced by record albums. Candy and bubble-gum purchases fade in favor of provocative perfumes. The boys become more interested in sports than in toy trucks. Muscle development takes precedence over bike riding. Boys even begin to acknowledge the existence of girls. With this discovery, clothes begin to mean more. Just a pair of jeans and a T-shirt are no longer enough. For both boys and girls, the mirror comes into an age of its own.

These are just a few of the changes you've started noticing in your children, the ones who have been model children through the fifth grade. Now these same children do or say things that puzzle you. You say, "They've never acted this way before!" "I'm beginning to think they don't even like me." "Why do they think I'm punishing them when I ask them to do something around the house?" They never before seemed to mind when you reminded them to brush their teeth, pick up their toys, hang up their clothes, wipe their shoes before coming into the house, wash their hands before coming to a meal, or shut the door when the air conditioner or furnace is on.

What is happening? At the beginning of this new period in their lives you need to face, deliberately and honestly, a difficult question: "Do I really love my teens?" You may respond, "What a silly question! They're mine, aren't they?" Yes, but do you love them enough to accept the changes that will take place in their lives? Do you have the time it takes to understand and work through "phase three"?

This understanding demands enormous amounts of unselfishness as far as your time is concerned. When they were small, your children needed you when they were sick, hungry, hurt, lonely, or angry. It will be no different now. They will still require your time, and that will not always be convenient for you.

Don't lose sight of why families were created in the first place. Families were instituted so that everyone could experience that great feeling of *belonging* somewhere, of being related to others, and of being a part of a group that gives each member a sense that people care. You can't afford to let this purpose get lost in the shuffle.

You have a demanding job. You've had one ever since

you gave birth to your first baby. Now your responsibility is to gradually start releasing your children from your grip, and to know when your hold on them should be completely relinquished. Perhaps you have ignored or disregarded the fact that the years with your children were coming to an end. It has been difficult to notice the changes that were going on because of the rapid pace you have kept as a parent. But your unawareness doesn't keep the changes from materializing.

There will always be a few teens who show only slight changes in their attitudes toward their parents during these turbulent years. While that group acknowledges the presence of their parents, the majority of teens may feel that they would like to apply vanishing cream to their parents. You notice this when you're with your teens in public. They insist on walking either three feet ahead of you or three feet behind you, mumbling, "You're not my mother," or "I'll bet there's no one else my age that goes to town with their parents!" They are totally destroyed socially if you touch them or show any signs of affection in public.

Another characteristic of phase three is the discovery that parents no longer have all the answers—in fact, they have *none* of the answers. Teens suddenly feel very knowledgeable, and parents are left bewildered by the fact that their teens think they have learned all the answers about life overnight. The answers parents do give are questioned and are often compared to the answers given by the friends (peers) of their teen-agers. Peer relationships form such a strong bond that they may outlast the United Nations or any other organized force in the world.

These peers will have an unequaled influence on your teens. When your teens are with their friends, you may witness an instant transformation. The teens who are quiet at home may be boisterous with their peers. The teens who only shrug when parents ask them questions are often the school's leading debaters. The teens who cannot decide what to wear to school will be elected class officers. The teens who rarely sing around the house will sing the leads in school musicals. If you tell your teens, "You look great," they'll respond, "Oh, you're just my mom." (Translated: "Your vote doesn't count.") But if they get the same compliment from one of their peers, they'll be elated for the next twenty-four hours.

Teen-agers have one foot in childhood and one foot in adulthood. They're at that in-between, uncertain age bracket, and they're not quite sure on which side of the bracket they belong. They have new feelings of distance from their parents. Figuratively, they sign their names to a Declaration of Independence, but they aren't quite sure what this new independence involves. To fulfill their new role, they will have to do lots of experimenting and thinking. This will take place in their own world of privacy —their room.

There may have been a time when your teens came directly home from school, and were ready to tell you everything that had happened while they were there. Now, instead of stopping to talk with you, they may go directly to their room and close the door. You'll wonder what they're doing in there, but instinct tells you that they need to be alone.

There is a desire for privacy in all of us. You have a need for privacy at various times during the day, and your teens are no different. They have the right to and the need for privacy as a means for discovering and cultivating who they are. This need for privacy is more intense in the teen-age years than in adulthood, and it gradually diminishes through the later years.

It is in the private domain of their rooms that teens are most alike. The walls and ceilings of the boys' rooms will display posters of attractive females. And the girls' rooms will exhibit posters of attractive males. They'll have their stereos, albums, radios, and tapes. Their bulletin boards will be full of mementos that have special meaning to them—clippings, awards, phone numbers, photos, and school-program booklets.

Changes Teens Notice

Maybe you think you're the only one noticing changes in your teens, but you're wrong. Your teens are acutely aware that they are changing, although they may not be quite sure why they're feeling different.

Their comments and questions about themselves give clues on how they feel about their changing personal appearance. "I'll bet you didn't wear this dumb shoe size when you were my age." "Do you think I'll get any taller?" "Is there anything I can do to keep my nose from looking so big?" "Just look at these legs!" "My ears look as if they've been put on upside down."

Relatives have an uncanny way of drawing out the things that teens are most sensitive about. You'll notice that they keep trying to find ways to avoid family gatherings, so they won't have to hear, "You sure have grown!" "How tall are you, anyway?" "You ought to put a brick on your head."

These teens are being reminded over and over that they're losing their childhood status. They had established their place in junior high school, but now they feel lost and unimportant around the seemingly sophisticated high-school upperclassmen. It's a bewildering time as reality intrudes and replaces all fanciful notions they may have had about growing up.

The girls have a gnawing desire to continue playing with their dolls, but they don't want their friends to know about it. When the desire overwhelms them, they try to find a secluded spot to play in. Eventually, they may make the final resolution and reluctantly pack the dolls away for the children they'll someday have. Then *their* daughters will go through this same process, although they will never fully understand *their* feelings, either.

The boys are no longer completely disgusted with girls. They don't know why, but they don't feel as comfortable climbing trees, wrestling, playing baseball, or riding bikes with girls. They're also finding out that it's much more fun to sit at ball games with boys their age, rather than with their parents.

These teens experience hurt more often and more deeply than when they were children. They hurt when they're discouraged or when they've been embarrassed. They hurt when a teacher causes them to lose face in front of their peers. It isn't like the hurt they felt as children. These new hurts are deeper and cannot be kissed away as they once were. You will hear statements from your teens that summarize all of this. "Mom, I am different than I used to be. I *am* trying to please you. Won't you accept me the way I am?"

The Beginning of Wisdom

So these teens are dealing with changes, and their parents must deal with accepting those changes. Why is it that parents do so well at accepting the changes that normally occur between babyhood and childhood, but balk when the same children continue to change throughout the teen years?

These changes need to be accompanied not only with acceptance but also with understanding. Granted, it is tricky to try to understand these teens who are still in the process of trying to understand themselves. But recognize that they are trying to communicate with you, asking for your patience. Whether they realize it or not, they are saying, "Love me anyway. Love me for what I am and for what I will someday become."

You must continue to develop the parental sixth sense of *awareness*. You began doing this years ago. When your children got hungry, you could heat a hot dog for them to eat and they would be satisfied. When they outgrew their clothing, you could replace it with clothing bought at a bargain-basement or a garage sale. You became instantly aware of these simple needs. Now, even though you are dealing with needs that are not as easily detected or understood, you can still rely on your parental instincts. But develop them!

Learn All You Can

Your teens cannot tell you how they are feeling. It's impossible to express oneself about something he's never before experienced. How do *you* verbalize something you don't understand? You can't! Teens can't!

So at this point, you begin learning all you can in order to successfully maneuver yourself and your teens through these changes. Make it a point to find out what is going on at school. Discover what excites, satisfies, frustrates, and intimidates your teens. Watch them yell at ball games. Listen to what they have to share at meal time. Decipher, with their help, "new" teen expressions, so you won't embarrass yourself—or them. Read books to encourage, enlighten, and strengthen you. Observe your teens' facial expressions and other body language. That can tell you the complete story of your teens' day.

Take time to check out their various moods. See if they're trying to disguise what they really feel. Feelings and moods will be communicated through the quickness or heaviness of their steps, the way they slam the car door, or the way they turn up the volume on their stereos.

These moods will remind you of your own teen years. But remember, the years between your teen-age experiences and those of your children are many. The two situations defy comparison. Besides, your teens will never welcome that worn-out phrase, "When *I* was a teen . . . ."

Get in Touch

It is compulsory for parents to occasionally become a part of their teens' world in order to view it from their vantage point. This is where active awareness begins. If you become so involved in your own world that you can't take the time to see and hear what's going on in theirs, you will not get any distinct clues about what your teens are saying and doing, and why they're reacting the way they are.

If you want to develop that sixth sense, you will have to recognize the value teens place on radios, stereos, movies, and teen magazines. You hear the radio click on to the favorite teen station first thing each morning as your teens wake up to it. The same musical beat is heard during breakfast and while the teens are getting ready for school. It continues as they walk out the door. The only brief interlude comes during the few steps before they make contact with the car radio.

Have you paid much attention to the words of the songs they're hearing? They aren't just listening to the rhythms—they know every word to every song. If you can't understand what words are being sung, open up one of your teen's albums. If you can get past the pictures, read some of the words. These songs are playing on the new emotional state present in your teens' lives—love. The themes are always built around love—the unfairness of it, the heartbreak of it, the innocence and tenderness of it. Your teens are reaching out into an area of life that's completely new and exciting to them. They are mentally fantasizing what love and life must mean.

Scan the newspaper. Read the description of some of the movies. Look at the long lines of teens waiting to get into the theaters. Why not join one of the lines? I am not suggesting that you make it a weekly habit to go to R-rated movies; one of them will probably be all you'll need to view to get the idea. But if you don't do this, how can you intelligently discuss them with your teens? You may feel that these kinds of movies are not ideal sources of entertainment, and this way you'll be able to say why. When the discussion comes up you won't have to hear, "You don't know what you're talking about." You *will* know what you're talking about. But be prepared—you will see and hear love expressed openly, passionately, and intimately. You will hear words that you thought were reserved only for privacy.

You'll see how movie producers play upon the emotions of a young audience that is not yet equipped to deal with what they are seeing and feeling. You will want to find a way to help your teens understand that this is not what love was intended to be, nor how life actually is. Your responsibility to your teens is to guide them to realize that what they're listening to and seeing does not deal with the complete meaning of love. The music makers and movie writers do not show the responsibilities that go with love. They fail to show the guilt and the frustrations people experience when love is misused. Your teens are being exposed to only one small segment of the meaning of love.

You'll do your best to get your teens to see the deeper values. But then it will be up to them to sort out what values they want to be included in their lives. It will be difficult to watch them floundering with their decisions. It will be frightening to see them making obvious mistakes. It will be disheartening to sense that your teachings and your beliefs are being temporarily pushed out of their lives. But don't give up!

Keep in Touch

Believe that the days of almost constant upsets are not going to last forever. You may need to write *"This Is Temporary"* on slips of paper and tape them on mirrors, above doors, at the stove, in the car, on top of your teens' stereos. After all, you can handle any situation—a week of rainy days, an overdrawn bank account, a bad cold—if you know it's temporary.

Even more reassuring is the knowledge that built into every parent's heart is an instinct that is always aware of their teen's needs. This awareness comes from genuine love. Reserve generous portions of this love for your teens —it will be the sustaining force throughout their lives. Love will overshadow anything you say or any mistakes you make. Even though at times love will not seem sufficient and though at times it won't or can't be expressed, it will always be present and working.

When you observe the lives of your teens and you think about all the things that might happen with them, it may seem like an endless television soap opera. Even though you don't know the outcome of this drama, keep in mind that you should never minimize what God can do in the lives of your teens or in your lives as their parents. With this assurance, you can walk in confidence through each day with your teens.

Are you ready to start the walk?

"Please Listen to Me"

In *The Informed Heart,* Dr. Bruno Bettelheim writes, "We are in great haste to send and receive messages from outer space. But so hectic and often so tedious are our days that many of us have nothing of importance to communicate to those close to us."[1]

Think of your family's schedules. They're awful, aren't they? You can't think of a day or night this week when there aren't "things" to be done. You've wondered if there will ever be an evening when all of your family can be at home at the same time. You don't have the nerve to say it out loud, but you've probably half-hoped for a power failure, a blizzard, an ice storm, gas rationing, or anything else it would take to slow the world down for a few hours so that you and your family can have some prime time with each other.

What is it in our make-up that causes us to have this need to communicate? Why do we need to feel free to ex-

1. Bruno Bettelheim, *The Informed Heart* (New York: Avon Books, 1971) p. vii.

press ourselves and to have people listen to us? Most of us know some of the results when people stop communicating. There is a lack of understanding, lack of listening, and lack of empathy.

Because communication is essential, teens and their parents may have to do some schedule-altering to begin to practice, and then to maintain, this idea of better communication within the family unit. Schedules don't automatically slow down, especially when there are teen-agers in the house. It takes planning, persistence, determination, willpower, stubbornness, and whatever else you can muster to help your family see the importance of spending time with each other. And, when everyone *is* together, encourage them to make an effort at communication.

Anyone will agree that smoke signals are out of date, telegrams are too impersonal, messages sent by homing pigeons are too impractical, and "by appointment only" is too formal. The kind of communicating I'm talking about is the core of living successfully with one another: the one-on-one. This is the kind that will take place when those involved have *understood* each other. Communication can't exist until understanding takes place.

When should good communication start? Obviously, it does not start when the children reach the teen years; it starts much sooner. My theory of when good communication should begin is rather homespun, but I hope you will recognize its wisdom.

When each of our babies was only a few hours old, we started holding her close to us and talking to her. It probably sounded foolish to outsiders, but we didn't have time to consider their opinions. The only response we hoped to receive from our babies was a smile, a "goo" or a "coo." That first response was important to us. Later, we created games with them, played on swing sets together, took walks, picnicked, and cuddled them at night as we told made-up stories. In all these activities, and many more, we were creating the atmosphere for communicating. We were making eye contact, touching each other, and hearing each other's voices.

I can't say that I knew the full implications of these activities at the time, but I can now verify that they started something special between us that has continued through the years. Our lines of communication have not always been perfect (they still aren't), but each of us has come to understand how vital and rewarding good communication is.

Interaction among family members takes time to develop. It isn't quite so difficult to plan this when the children are small. But teens have ways of complicating even simple schedules. Homework, sports, debate, drama, music, partying, dating, and cruising—all of these steal time from families. It wouldn't be fair or healthy for you to expect or demand that your teens remove all of these things from their lives. They have their place, but so does developing a strong home base. You cannot leave it up to your teens to see the value of communication. It is *your* responsibility to let them know that communication takes everyone's cooperation. And it can't be done if schedules remain crammed.

Because of the intensified activities and demands on your teens, they could very quickly become strangers to you. Sometimes, even now, the only visible evidence that you have of their existence is clothes scattered around their rooms—or *by* the clothes hamper. There's an occasional school book on the kitchen table, an empty potato-chip bag, single socks and shoes around the living room, and half-eaten sandwiches in odd places. This hectic atmosphere, coupled with their impossible schedules, doesn't mean that they no longer want you to be an integral part of their lives. They don't need you as much as they once did, but it is evident that they still occasionally need the security blanket of home.

Some of the most meaningful occurrences within families have small beginnings. Tell your family how important you feel it is that they spend more time together. Simply begin by asking your family to cooperate at least once a week for a month. Then at the end of the month evaluate how each family member feels about better communication.

TIME OUT

Sit down as a family and ask all members to write out a list of the activities in which they're involved. Put a "1" beside the things that must be done, a "2" by the things that they enjoy but are considered "extras," and a "3" by the things in which they aren't particularly interested.

After all have checked their lists, begin to discuss what can be left out of each person's schedule in order to have more time together as a family.

Your goal is not only to try to spend more time together, but also to decide what you're going to do when you *are* together.

How Good Communication Starts

Many parents say, "Our teens don't tell us anything! If we learn something about them, it's usually by accident or from some person we hardly know." How do you get teens to talk to you?

Before you set up any strategies, go back one step. Be honest. How easy is it for you and your spouse to talk to each other? Is it difficult to relate to one another? If there is a problem of communication in your home, it could be rooted in your inability to express yourselves to each other as husband and wife. Consider this Time Out with your spouse in order to rate yourselves.

TIME OUT

Share with your spouse three statements that you believe are true about him or her. Then share three statements that you believe are true about yourself.

These are to be things you believe are true right now. Do not include things from the past. Say, "At this time I believe _____ about you." If one of the truths happens to be negative, put into constructive words. Ask your spouse to follow the same procedure with you.

Each of you may want to comment on specific things the other has shared.

Try this exercise once a week to see if you're receiving clear messages from each other.

When you think about communication between you and your spouse, don't think only about verbal communication. Think about all the messages you transmit to each other through embraces, looks, and body language, as well as through spoken messages. Until my husband and I saw the importance of communicating with each other, our children were being cheated out of this vital area of family life. Communicating genuine love is one of the greatest and most lasting gifts you can ever give your family. It will become a strong, determining force in your teens' adult lives.

Communication brings about healing when wounds have been received inside—as well as outside—the home. When you give time to your teens, they will open up secret doors in their lives so you can see why they think, speak, and live the way they do. You'll begin to understand their motives, their shortcomings, their values, their questions, and their concerns. With this knowledge, your faith in these teens will help you see their special personalities. Your love for them will exceed your doubts about them. Your trust will reduce your worry.

Perhaps you're already fortunate enough to have good rapport with your teens. Even so, it is still necessary to check in from time to time to see where you're standing with each other. Try to find out how much time is actually being spent with each family member. You may want to evaluate communication weekly or monthly with questions such as:

1. How many minutes a day do you think you are spending with each family member?
2. Have you had a good talk with someone in the family this past week? When was it? Who was it with?
3. Is there a certain member of the family with whom you find it difficult to talk with? If so, the two of you should discuss how you might better communicate.

Teens, like their parents, will communicate in ways that are most comfortable for them. I don't know of a more relaxed, informal time for conversation than at meal times. I know you're already saying, "We're never all together for a meal!" There may occasionally be a legitimate reason for skipping a family meal, but if this is the only time the family has to talk together, you all should decide what's more important—family time or outside activities.

Set a goal for everyone to be together for a meal at least once a week. Each member may have to cancel something, but you'll find that the results are so rewarding when family communication becomes a priority.

TIME OUT

During a meal, without announcing what you're doing, make a point of listening to the tones of voice of those talking. Later, relate to your family your impressions of what you heard.

Note if most of the conversations were negative or critical, or if one person was doing all the talking. Ask your family if they agree or disagree with your observation.

This would be a good time for your family to decide how these situations can be corrected. Then concentrate on implementing the family suggestions.

Encourage others to listen at various times and report on what they hear. Make sure the "good times" are also observed and shared.

When one of our daughters was in high school, she taught me a lesson about the importance of my tone of voice. She had the habit of coming home from school and turning the volume dial of her stereo as high as it would go in order to "catch all the vibes," as she put it. For several years I felt I would have the stamina to outlast the intensity of that sound, but on one particular day, I felt that one of us was going to have to surrender. And, as unfair as it might sound, it wasn't going to be me!

I was in the kitchen preparing dinner, and I yelled, "Turn that thing down!" When the volume remained the same (she probably wasn't able to hear me yelling), I dug my heels into the carpet and stomped down the hall. When I was halfway to her room I noticed there were no more sounds coming from it. However, I kept up my oratory. To my surprise, she was smiling when I entered her room. How do you continue a verbal outburst in front of a smile? I said, "Thank you!" and left.

A few minutes later, she called me into her room. She turned on her tape recorder and played back her latest recording. She had taped my voice and my steps as I marched down the hall toward her room. She had captured every harsh inflection in my voice. Even my footsteps sounded angry. After we laughed together, there was really nothing I could say—but I had plenty to think about.

I'm not saying that it was wrong for me to be angry. But I believe I learned that I could get my point across just as effectively without losing control. After that incident, I think I began improving in that area. Someday, I plan to ask my daughter if she ever erased that tape!

The reactions we get from our teens *are* to some extent a result of the tone of our voices. The familiar maxim is really true: "It's not *what* you say, it's *how* you say it that makes the difference."

TIME OUT

Sit down with your teens. Say something to them that you tell them often, perhaps something such as, "I think it's time you cleaned your room." Ask them to repeat exactly what you said, imitating your voice, facial expressions, body position, and any other gestures you've made.

If you hear your teens saying exactly what you thought you said, and implied, say so. If that isn't how you thought you said it, or implied it, tell them. Ask them how you could have spoken differently to get the message across the way you intended it to be received.

Reverse the role with them.

I have always felt that the most critical time for family communication is at the beginning and the end of each day. Mornings set the mood for the day, and evenings give family members a chance to repair any breakdowns in communication that have occurred through the day.

There aren't many tasks that require more energy and determination than getting everyone up "on the right side of bed" each morning, especially when everyone is rushing to get to school or work on time. If you're not sure that their minds come to breakfast with their bodies, you might consider this Time Out.

TIME OUT

In the morning have each family member (you, too) write a short description of his or her mood. That evening talk about those moods, discussing how each member can be sensitive to the others' moods.

Creating the Atmosphere for Communication

It takes a great deal of unselfishness and time to help teen-agers grow. It would be extremely easy to let your teens go their way while you go yours. And on the surface, it appears that's exactly what teens want. Teens don't expect their parents to go to everything they're involved in. They may even ask their parents to stay home from some of their activities. Just think how tempting it would be: The house would certainly be quieter; there would be several hours of uninterrupted time every day to do whatever you'd like. But there is value in participating in at least *some* activities with your teens, if for no other reason than to have common ground on which to meet.

Try to get permission to enter your teen's room some evening. If permission is granted, you can use your time together by sitting on his or her bed, or stretching out beside him and letting a variety of subjects evolve. Of course, there will also be times when your teens will value having some quiet moments—and so will you. But against a backdrop of communication, you'll be able to show them how these times can revitalize and refresh them.

Or, how about taking a walk together? I am an avid, brisk daily walker, and I've found that problems that loom large before I start my walk are reduced in size by the time I've finished. I reasoned that if walking did *me* so much good, I wanted to share this walk with my daughter. When we first started walking together we didn't do much talking; we just concentrated on keeping a steady pace. The talking came later. After one summer of this, I evaluated the time we had spent together. I was pleased that she had shared with me many of the things she was working out on her own.

Walking in the country or sitting beside a quiet stream together is a cheap but priceless therapy. There may be no need to talk, and that's fine. If you or your teens want to talk, it may be about subjects that would never be brought up at any other time. You'll be surprised to hear your teens come out with conversation-starters such as, "Mom, when you were young did you. . . ?" or "When I was little did I. . . ?" You will both recall some pleasant memories. There may be no special reason for getting out like this, but since your teens experience so few minutes of "nothingness," it could be a way of restoring and reactivating their minds and bodies—yours, too! So head for the hills!

One father of a ninth-grade girl noticed that his daughter had practically stopped talking to him. He mentioned this to his wife, who said, "Whose fault do you think it is?" That evening he invited his daughter out for dinner. Later they drove to a river close to their houe and took a long walk. During that time they decided that he would pick her up from school twice a week in order to give them some extra time together.

Every family has suffered together through term-paper deadlines, art projects, or test-cramming sessions. There needs to be a break from even these tense situations. Ask your teens to go out for a soda. It's a whole new atmosphere. The quality of conversation changes, and even though neither one of you can express it, it becomes a satisfying time together.

Conscientious parents don't intentionally try to keep from spending time with their teens. All of us, however, need to become aware of communication opportunities that are there throughout the day. Once we recognize them, we can take advantage of them.

It Isn't Too Late to Start!

I have already mentioned that good communication between parents and their children probably starts at birth. This doesn't offer much encouragement to parents who get only shrugs, grunts, or stares from their teens. It's a universal plague among parents to start analyzing this and to start asking, "What did we do wrong? When did we go wrong?" We answer ourselves by saying, "We'll have to learn to live with it. They've never talked to us and they never will. It's too late to change anything now."

Once you voice these negative thoughts, join the positive forces. Communication, or lack of it, is learned, and anything that is learned can be changed! Maybe you haven't communicated with your teens, but things can change and you can initiate that change. You and your spouse will have to take the initial steps and suggest changes you want to occur.

TIME OUT

Write out the basic things you would like to give your teens. Discuss them with each other. Include creating good communication with each family member.

After you have discussed your list with each other, sit down with your teens and talk to them about the basics you've listed. Ask them if they feel you are communicating these ideas to them.

Encourage them to comment on how well they feel the family is communicating with each other.

Emphasize this desire for better communication with your family. Help them realize that things can change, and that it'll take everyone's cooperation to make the changes. If you invite free expression, expect to get it. One mother said that she and her daughter have to have an argument before thay can have a civil conversation, especially if they have opposing views. Some conversations might end in an argument, with everyone leaving before things can be resolved. The family may begin to avoid anything that implies unpleasantness. If this happens, problems will not be solved.

Families need to communicate until solutions or compromises are reached. At first, family members may become upset, frustrated, or confused, but eventually they will learn to rationalize and reason. Some problems will take a long time to correct. When this is true, you may have to continue the same conversation at another time.

I don't want to emphasize only the problems families have. Family members must also learn to help each other express the positive feelings they have for each other. To give a compliment or to say, "I love you," is not an extinct practice. It might seem awkward at first, but it is easier with practice.

After you have had this first meeting with your family, leave some time for apologies, awareness of each other's needs, and renewals of family relationships. The time of commitment may involve your saying, "I'm sure our family will never be nominated for the Nobel Peace Prize, but I'm willing to help make the situation better. Will you help?"

On the Level

People don't often say it anymore, but you've heard, "Come on, level with me." Perhaps one of the greatest problems we encounter with our teens is that we don't recognize the value of being completely honest with them.

It was never difficult for me to do this with my children when they were younger. The questions they asked then—"Will you play dolls with me?" "Will you come out and swing with me?" "Will you read me a book?"—were answered by "Yes," "No," or "In a minute."

But what happened to my straightforward answers when my teenagers' questions descended upon me? Somewhere along the way, I stopped leveling with them. After examining my reactions, I believe I know why I found it difficult to be completely honest with our teenagers.

An element of fear kept me from being completely honest with our teens. I was not afraid of *them*. I was afraid that I would not make wise enough judgments when I answered their questions. I would find myself looking too far into their futures and wondering how my answers would affect their lives. Therefore, I distrusted my judgments.

Sometimes I would totally agree with what our teens were saying, doing, or asking. I was generous with my honesty at that point. But when I disagreed with what they were saying, doing, or asking, I became unsure about what I should say. My love for them would not allow me to look objectively at what they were asking of me. They were asking me to level with them if I didn't agree with them, if it meant disappointing them, or if they became frustrated or angry with me.

Think back on the times when you knew you would have to be totally honest with your teens. You wanted to be both honest and fair. You didn't want to disappoint them; you didn't want them to resent you. Most of all, you thought they might not love you for doing what you knew you must do. This last consideration becomes an unjust fear. We love these struggling human beings so much that we want to demonstrate the essence of that love. Our common sense has to tell us that demonstrating love does not always mean agreeing with our teens. Since we don't know how our teens will react, we begin to recognize that honesty carries a high degree of risk —that what we say may have uncertain results.

I always felt safe about being completely honest in pleasant situations with our teens. But I couldn't find that same openness when we were guarding opposite goal posts. This frustrated me. I can only surmise how much it frustrated them.

Where or when do parents start being completely honest with teens? Some things have to start with apologies. Admit that you haven't been able to level with them about certain things. Admit that you aren't a perfect parent. Admitting to your imperfections may be the thing that will make a stronger alliance between you and your teens. I believe that people trust humanness more than they do perfection.

Both parents and teens should understand that honesty should not be so brutal that it destroys the self-image of the one with whom you're leveling. The truth should be delivered with tact, should be uplifting, and should carry with it constructive criticism. Truths should be told only to help the person for whom they are intended, or to strengthen family relationships. Sometimes criticism should not be immediate, or it will merely make a situation worse.

If you expect instant results from leveling—don't. In time, honesty will create a trust between each of you that will last forever. I couldn't have written about this particular fringe benefit of parenting until the children were older, because I didn't know the dynamic results of leveling. I know now, and that trust has become just one more gift we are able to share together.

Here are some Time Outs that could help you begin leveling with your teens.

TIME OUT

Ask your teens what they know about your feelings. You may start by saying, "How do you think I feel about (mention a particular situation)?" After they comment, let them know if they have correctly assessed your feelings. Give them the same opportunity to tell you about some of their feelings.

TIME OUT

Tell your family something about yourself that they wouldn't know unless you told them. This might include things that embarrass you, make you happy, make you angry, or give you pleasure; ways you feel toward certain family members; secret ambitions; or habits you're trying to break. Give them time to comment. Allow them this same opportunity.

TIME OUT

Sit facing another family member. While you're looking at each other, silently answer these questions: "Does this person remind you of anyone?" "How do you feel about *that* person?" "Are your feelings negative or positive?"

Now tell each other the thoughts you had.

This Time Out can make you aware of how you feel about certain family members. Use these questions to evaluate your thoughts: Did this Time Out make you uneasy or scared? Were you excited to tell your partner the things you were thinking?

If your feelings were mostly negative, you may have wanted to hide how you actually felt. If you were scared, that kept you from telling much. If you thought you had to measure your words, try to decide what made you hesitant about saying what you wanted to say.

If you had many negative thoughts, you may have to find ways of working on your relationship with that person.

Teens will not have any difficulty relating their thoughts about their brothers or sisters. It may be extremely hard or almost impossible for them to be completely honest about their feelings toward their parents. Make it comfortable for them to share their feelings.

The first time your family tries one of these Time Outs may be awkward or embarrassing. But keep trying. When you've been able to risk sharing your thoughts and feelings, many barriers to communication begin to break down.

As those barriers fall, parents will find that communication alone may not produce accord. For example, we parents, through the years, have built up strong convictions, or values, that we want to pass on to our teens. But when we tell our teens about these values, we find our teens disagree with us.

How should parents respond to this? At this point, parents must add a new dimension to leveling—negotiating or compromising. Don't adults negotiate when they can't completely agree with each other? Although the idea might be new to you, aren't you dealing with adults now?

Whether or not our teens look like, act like, or think like adults, they are in the process of becoming adults, and we must treat them as such. When we raise our sights to their new level, we can simplify many situations. A lifelong trust will develop because we have been willing to compromise with our teens and deal with them as adults.

If you have always done this with your children, I commend you. If you haven't and you would like to begin, I wonder if you are brave enough to allow your teens to level with you. You may hear some unpleasant things. It's painful to hear about some of our weaknesses. But your teens must feel just as comfortable leveling with you as you do with them. This liberty allows teens and parents to solve misunderstandings and disagreements. It may also precipitate expressions of appreciation that you never expected from those frivolous teens.

The development of such honesty within families is the goal of Virginia Satir, a family therapist, who writes, "I would like to see each human being value and appreciate himself, feel whole, creative, competent, healthy, rugged, beautiful, and loving."[2] You say that this is idealistic; we have to face reality. I say that even though we cannot reach this stage of family perfection, we can at least strive for it.

You Got Your Ears On?

Nothing is required—except time—when we are asked to listen. At times listening becomes one of the

2. Virginia Satir, *Peoplemaking* (Palo Alto, CA: Science and Behavior Books, Inc.), 1972, p. 79.

hardest things that parents of teen-agers must do. The scene becomes dramatic in the later teen years when issues become complex; decisions, sometimes life-changing; and mistakes, tragic.

When your teens start sharing confidences with you, you'll know you understand them, because your stomach starts doing unexpected things. You don't want to show what you feel because you're afraid your teens will stop talking. These teens cause you to reflect on the days when you were either suppressing or expressing similar feelings. You have the solutions to their problems—now. You didn't then. They don't either.

When your teens talk to you, they don't necessarily want to hear your opinions. They're only asking that you listen. Listening is one of the greatest contributions you can add to your teens' lives. When you listen, you are letting them reveal who they are, not what you want them to do or be. You're helping them solve certain situations, but not necessarily the way you would solve them. Listening lends them the support they need. If you listen to them, they won't feel that they have to go to someone outside the family for support.

A teen-ager came to me crying out for someone to listen to her. Her parents worked so their children could have "things." This girl wore expensive clothes, had a sizable allowance, and owned a car. She came to me one day and said, "I don't need all these 'things!' I just want some of my mother's time." She cried; I felt like crying with her. Maybe she couldn't say exactly what she felt, but she wanted her mother to take time to listen to her. The solution to her problem came the next year. She was pregnant, married, and divorced, within the same year. She then moved back home to be with her parents. She told me later, "My mother and I have never been so close. We seem to have more time for each other." What she had been asking for all along was free—time.

I don't feel that all teens would take such drastic measures to get their parents to listen to them. I share this story to show you the dynamic place that listening has in the lives of our teens. They may not be able to express or even recognize that need, but it is present, and it's important at this particular time in their lives.

Teens do have things to share and they need someone with whom to share them. They need available parents! One teen said, "I wish I could find one person who would take the time to show he really cares how I feel."

If your teens ask you to listen to them, they aren't always expecting you to give them answers. They want you to hear them out—completely, with no interruptions. Unconsciously, we are so anxious to offer advice from our vast field of adult knowledge that we cut our teens off before they can finish talking. One of our daughters chose to discuss something with me. I immediately began a monologue that must have seemed endless to her. She interrupted as politely as she could and said, "Mom, I don't always expect you to talk after I've told you something. I'll have to work out some of these things for myself." I had thought it was my parental duty to talk after she had told me something. I was relieved to know that I didn't have to give answers or suggestions unless she asked for them.

I keep hearing teens say, "Listen to me. Just listen. I may not have all the answers yet, but I feel better because I've been able to talk to someone." If we can refrain from excessive talking, we're permitting our teens full expression. This calms them and helps them rationalize and view situations from different perspectives.

A mother said that after she had asked her daughter four times what her plans were for the week, the teen responded, "You never listen, do you, Mom?" We look at our teens while they're talking. We see their mouths moving. We hear sounds coming from their throats, but our minds have an innate tendency to do other things while they're talking. If we're lucky we can catch just enough of what they're saying to throw in an occasional "uh-huh," "yes," or "I see." We also may be deciding what we'll fix for the evening meal, thinking about the phone calls we've had, or making final plans for one of the monthly meetings over which we preside.

Some teens were asked, "How do you know when your parents aren't listening to you?" They came up with the following answers: "If they're not looking at me." "If they're reading the newspaper while I'm talking." "If they keep vacuuming or cooking and say, 'Go ahead, I can hear you.'" Then the teens were asked, "How do you know when your parents are listening to you?" Most of them said, "If they stop what they're doing when I'm talking to them."

A two-year-old boy started to say something to his mother, who was busy washing dishes. He walked over to her and said, "Hold me." After she picked him up, he pulled her face around to his and kept his hands on her face until he was through talking. Would it be necessary for your teens to pull your face around to theirs so they know that they have your undivided attention when they need to talk with you? It does seem that there are times when they ask for your attention at the most inopportune moments—when you're in the middle of preparing a difficult recipe, when there are only five minutes left of a movie you've been watching for three hours, when you're already fifteen minutes late for a meeting, or when your mind stops functioning at 10:00 P.M. and they're pushing you to help them solve a real-life drama at 11:00 P.M.

There are times when saying, "Wait a minute," is permissible, but not if you say it so often that the teens completely close you out of their lives. How much time is required for listening? How many interruptions from your private thoughts, personal achievements, and daily routines does it require? If good communication is accepted in your household, the family members will take it for granted that there will be some listening time included in every day.

Write out a checklist of your weekly activities to see which ones include your teens. Then decide how many opportunities you have to listen to them while you're together. This could reveal what kind of grade you should give yourself as a listener. If you deserve a failing grade, it would be worth your time to revise your list and include time to listen to your teens.

It's essential that your teens feel that you have time to hear what has happened to them through the day. Everything that affects their lives away from home is going to affect you and the rest of the family. When they come home in an untouchable mood, you can't afford to shrug them off by thinking, "It's just their age." Maybe they've had to hold back on certain strong feelings at school. They've been disappointed (I didn't pass the test), embarrassed (I dropped my tray in the cafeteria), insulted (someone called me clumsy), or left out (everyone got invited but me). When they get home they can release their feelings because they know they'll have someone to listen to them.

Your teens may be so upset that they won't be rational. They may cry or use language you're not prepared to hear. Listen to them, but don't get upset yourself. It'll be a matter of minutes or hours before they're back in control of themselves. While you're still fretting about what they've told you, they have forgotten this crisis and are braced for the next one.

If each person needs to have someone listen to him, isn't it logical that parents should be aware of this need? Parents can't measure the time that will be involved in listening. Some of the things your teens ask you to listen to will be as brief as a television commercial. Parents who aren't night people may be asked to listen during the hours of the late late show. Although you'll have to use eye drops first thing the next morning, and you know the day will seem extremely long before you can crawl wearily into bed once more, you've taken the time to listen. This is another form of love you give to your teens—not a form you can easily define, but one your teens can readily understand.

The Silent Treatment

I've already said that one of the hardest things parents are asked to do is to listen to their teens without giving advice. The hardest thing parents experience is when their teens don't want to talk or when they refuse to talk.

This doesn't necessarily mean that communication is in trouble. It may mean that you must awaken your sixth sense again to understand that some communication will be nonverbal. If I had known how normal this was, I could've saved miles of walking back and forth across the floor, as well as the expense of having to replace the carpet. I finally had to confront myself and realize that I wouldn't be included in our teens' every thought. As I walked, I rationalized that this was actually a healthy sign. I was doing something worthwhile. I was allowing our teens to work things out for themselves. They didn't need my help.

By allowing these silent treatments, we were encouraging our teens to develop a more independent level of functioning. I believe that parents who find it impossible to allow their children to have some interests of their own, without being a constant piece of their lives, are unconsciously fostering dependence.

It might be easier to understand nonverbal communication by picturing a familiar family scene. Think of one of those awful weeks when your preschoolers were inside all week because of bad weather or sickness, and your husband was out of town. When you knew he would be home, you met him at the door with your car keys in your hand. All you could manage to say was, "I have to get away for a while." You couldn't tell him why you had to get away. You just knew you had to go. If you and I have had or still have times when we can't verbally express ourselves, how can we expect our teens to verbalize everything?

Teens need time alone in order to reintegrate. Those

silent times behind closed doors in their rooms allow them to do that. This solitude will help them work out their inner battles. They may not know how to tell you that sometimes they do not want to share their feelings with you. Respecting their privacy will relieve some of the discomfort teens might experience. Let them know it's all right to say, "I don't want to talk right now. I may later, but I don't now." This doesn't mean they don't value you, so don't feel guilty when they choose not to talk to you.

If no one's talking, how can you know that communication hasn't stopped? Facial expressions, body positions, breathing tempos, and muscle tones are all nonverbal communication. Be aware of these nonverbal clues. It doesn't take a great deal of intelligence to discover how serious situations are when your teens have scowls embedded in their foreheads, are on the brink of tears, mutter in undistinguishable language, slam the door, throw gravel as they back the car out of the driveway, or play the piano, stereo, or radio at volumes that defy the sound barrier.

A parent's recourse at these times is to not pry and to do something else. I find that when I'm busy with other matters, I'm not mentally solving their problems about which I know nothing.

From time to time, I have encouraged our daughters to write about their feelings. I stipulate that I will not trespass on what they've written. You probably won't have to encourage it, but let them know it's all right to use strong language and to write exactly how and what they're feeling. They may break a few pencil points in the process. Later they may want to destroy what they have written or they may reread it and evaluate their feelings.

You may hesitate to suggest this to your teens because it might lead to unexpected results. For example, one evening I came home and found the following note that one of our teens had written: "Mom, I've gone somewhere for the night. I have a problem I have to work out. I'll be home tomorrow. Don't worry." What was wrong with that kid? I went back to pacing the carpet and rationalizing again, because it was going to be a long night. The threshold of pain was reduced when a friend of our daughter's called during the evening and told us where our daughter was.

Our daughter did come home the next day, just as she said she would. She didn't have her problem worked out, but she was trying. At that point I secretly questioned her methods. Several years later I understood that this was the only way she knew how to begin solving her problem. She had not been able to express exactly how she felt. When she had tried to talk to me, I couldn't be objective, so she left her home surroundings to struggle with the problem alone. It hurts to know that in order for your teens to achieve adulthood, they have to experience some painful, lonely hours where you aren't included.

I liked this idea of writing so much that I followed my own advice and began expressing things to our daughters that I probably wouldn't have done otherwise. How would your teens react if you brought them breakfast in bed with notes on the tray that said, "I'm proud of you," or "You're special in my life"? What's wrong with notes stuck in their school books, pinned to their pillows, taped to the steering wheel?

There may come a day when you'll find notes from your teens in obscure places: "Mom, you're neat!" or "Sorry I kept you up late last night. Thanks for staying up with me till I got all those things out of my system." And you may receive that special note that only a teen could get by with, "You're a great mom, even though you're over the hill."

Teens, like their parents, need time alone. They can also do an about-face and have a strong desire to be with you. They want you to share a part of their lives, although they may want you to share it in total silence. They want to feel your touch. They will probably never say, "I need you to hold me." You'll just know it's necessary and appropriate.

One dad found himself alone with his teen-age daughter, who had just come home from school crying. She ran into the house, went straight to her room, and continued crying. Her dad had always relied on his wife at times like this because he felt he never had the right words to say. He did the only thing he knew to do. He sat down beside his daughter and held her close until she stopped crying.

Remember how, when your children were small, they enjoyed being held close to you? They didn't need your touch just when they were hurt. Anytime you opened your arms to them, they'd accept your invitation and come running to you. When children become teen-agers, they don't outgrow their need to be touched. If this satisfied them in their childhood, why should we unconsciously eliminate it during the teen years? It doesn't take a tremendous amount of energy or creativity to give teens a handshake, a pat on the back, or a hug. These expressions are never meaningless. Although your teens may continue to suffer in silence, for some reason it does give them a measure of relief to feel your arms around them.

"You've Got Wrinkles in Your Earlobes"

One evening I was preparing dinner. My husband and one of our daughters were talking. I heard her say, "Dad, did you know you have wrinkles in your earlobes?" They started laughing and continued talking. I slowed down my dinner preparation. I wanted to give them time to talk. It gave me time to reflect and to realize that my husband understood how important it was to build strong relationships with each of our daughters. He played with them, read to them, shared his childhood experiences with them, explained things to them, and taught them to tie their shoes and ride bicycles. He helped them make their dreams come true. He experienced all the hundreds of things that go into years of growth when children are around.

I have seen my husband sitting with our teens in complete silence. I have heard him talking to them. I know these times have become precious memories to him and to our daughters. It has been especially good for me to know that he and I have shared the responsibility of building good communication.

I believe that communication is the greatest factor in successful family living. Because of its value, all of us must take time to work at it and develop it.

"Your Wife Is Driving Me Crazy"

He was seventeen years old, and his mother had just said to him, in one breath, "Change that dirty shirt, and be sure you wash your hands before you come to dinner." He found his father and said quietly but firmly, "Your wife is driving me crazy!"

I assume that similar statements had been aimed at this young man for several years. But now, as a teenager, he resented being told to do the same things that he had been told to do when he was younger. If his dad had asked him why these requests irritated him, he probably couldn't have said why. He just knew it bothered him to hear them day after day.

We parents need extraordinary insight to learn that our children will eventually become totally independent of us. In most cases, independence creeps into our lives so subtly that we don't recognize it when it finally stands before us.

The steps toward independence during those childhood years should have been clear to me, but my busy days kept me from seeing the progression. My journal entries could have looked like this:

Today,
> He clamped his mouth shut and refused strained spinach.
> He pushed my hand away while I was trying to feed him.
> He let go of my hand and walked alone.
> He tried to put on his own socks and shoes.
> He didn't want to hold my hand when we crossed the street.
> He wanted to choose the clothes he'd wear.
> He got tired of hearing me remind him to brush his teeth and eat his vegetables.
> He tried to break the habit of kissing me good-night and good-by.

You see? The progression was clear. I didn't resent any of these actions. My children were actually leaving me with fewer responsibilities. So why did I build such a case out of changes that took place when they were teens?

I have examined the process of becoming independent as it relates to our teens—they should be allowed gradually to become free without interference and opposition. But I wonder if we as parents oppose our teens' freedom. We don't follow the rules of the game. The rules call for unselfishness, relinquishing control, and consenting to complete independence from us. We know the rules, yet we find ourselves opposing them.

We've already seen that independence is necessary and normal. That sounds easy enough. The hard part comes when we need the wisdom to know how much independence we should allow our teens to have and when we should allow it. Too much too soon could be disastrous. Never to allow independence to develop is equally disastrous.

Independence is so important that we need all the help we can get in understanding its value. I believe that helping teens grow is such a difficult task that we need a higher source to help us know when to intervene in our teens' actions and when to allow them to have total responsibility for their actions. All parents of teens should know the following Bible verse:

> If you want to know what God wants you to do, ask him, and he will gladly tell you, for he is always ready to give a bountiful supply of wisdom to all who ask him; he will not resent it (James 1:5, LB).

If you haven't yet asked for wisdom, I'd suggest that you start now.

Sloan Wilson, in *What Shall We Wear to This Party?*, graphically summarizes the dilemma parents face:

> The hardest part of raising children is teaching them to ride bicycles. A father can either run beside the bicycle or stand yelling directions while the child falls. A shaky child on a bicycle for the first time needs both support and freedom. The realization that this is what the child will always need can hit hard.[1]

I wish I could have had access to that quote years ago. I would have been tempted to stamp it on my forehead, engrave it on a bracelet, or etch it onto my heart as a reminder to give both support and freedom to our daughters.

Elasticity is involved in this unfolding drama of independence. Teens bounce back and forth from childhood to adulthood, and parents are responsible for maintaining a balance between the two. Teens resolve to obtain complete independence from their parents. Parents must resolve to allow that.

I hope this chapter helps parents understand why it's

1. Sloan Wilson, *What Shall We Wear to This Party? The Man in the Gray Flannel Suit Twenty Years Before and After* (New York: Arbor House, 1976), p. 141.

necessary for teens to sometimes push against the limits of home and society, why it's important for parents to release their teens, and how they can release their teens successfully.

Christening Independence

For several years, most of you have had a Camelot relationship with your children. Now a different relationship exists. At this stage parents are no longer omnipotent. Teens no longer need a fantasy of perfect parents—the ones who had always outmaneuvered any impossible situation in the world. These teens have started moving out from their parents, getting opinions, instructions, and ideas from everywhere and everyone except from their parents.

Take time to reflect on some changes you've noticed. Remember how your children used to look forward to your coming to school on visiting day? Now they would seek lifelong asylum if you appeared anywhere on the school grounds. They would rather die than have you call a teacher to discuss a problem they have.

Another change concerns the elements of privacy and secrecy. Before this, your teens told you everything that had happened during the day, from vividly describing what they found in their food at the school cafeteria to naming which teachers they saw smoking in the prohibited areas. Now you don't hear nearly all of these details and you might not hear any of them.

You find yourself hesitating to greet your teens when they come in from school. You're not sure whether a handshake, a kiss, or no greeting at all is acceptable. There's no time for a kiss good-morning, good-night, or good-by. You had honestly felt—until now—that this particular ritual would last forever.

Your teens make it clear how they feel about going on vacations with the family. When they were younger, vacations always spelled excitement for them. They would pass away the miles by playing travel games, doing simple crafts, or singing with the rest of the family. Now, a hand, connected to a long arm, comes from the back seat and automatically turns on the radio. One father said that he was able to handle only so much of "their kind" of music on long trips. Now the family listens to "their kind" of music for thirty minutes, then to "his kind" for thirty minutes, and then observes thirty minutes of silence.

Other changes occur. Teen-age girls become fashion experts. Mothers are no longer equal to the task of laying out clothes for school. A mother cannot keep up with all of the new trends. One mother said that her daughter showed her the latest hair style. "Mom, all the girls are wearing their hair this way." The mother's silent reaction was, "I thought it was a condition they were trying to clear up."

Daughters not only observe themselves in full-length mirrors, but they also start to examine their mothers. They ask such questions as, "Mom, are you sure that hair style is the most becoming for you?" or "Have you ever thought about wearing pantyhose with tummy control?" You wonder what you've done to deserve all of this special attention. Instead of trying to find the answers, you learn to live with the reasons they might have for asking these loaded questions.

These teens are moving away from their parents. They're expanding their world, and opinions from home are filed away under "A" for ancient history. These moving-out years are not years of open defiance. This sentence demands to be written twice: Teen years are not years of open defiance.

I cannot believe that the majority of teens intentionally hurt their parents or oppose their parents' views for the sake of being difficult or different. Because we don't fully understand what our teens are going through, we become frustrated by seeming indifference, rejection, and rebellion.

In *P.E.T., Parent Effectiveness Training,* Dr. Thomas Gordon made these comments about rebellion and hostility at this stage of development:

> [The teen-ager] is no longer controlled by his parents' rewards because he doesn't need them as much, and he is immune to threats of punishment because there is little they can do to give him pain or strong discomfort. The typical adolescent behaves as he does because he has acquired enough strength and resources to satisfiy his own need and enough of his own power so that he need not fear the power of his parents.[2]

Dr. Gordon also writes that if parents would rely less on power to influence their children, there would be little for their children to rebel against when they become teen-agers.

I believe our teens rebel not out of defiance, but out of an inborn desire for freedom. I have said that this development of independence is elastic. When your teens show that they want to do things on their own, they don't mean that they want to abandon their parents immediately and completely. You'll need wisdom to know when to stand apart from your teens and when to stand close enough for them to reach out to you, if necessary.

I haven't always agreed with everything I've seen our teens doing, but neither have I disagreed with everything I've seen them doing. The beauty of having graduated two teens into the adult world is that I can now see them relating to me in their independent lifestyles. Their ways of life are not in complete accord with my way of life—they shouldn't be—but I continue to make an honest effort to accept their way of life, and I hope they try to accept mine.

Independence is inevitable. Its progress demands phenomenal patience and supreme wisdom. It isn't quite

2. Thomas Gordon, *P.E.T., Parent Effectiveness Training: The Tested New Way to Raise Responsible Children* (New York: New American Library, 1975), p. 172.

so overpowering when you know the results that can come from it.

To Be or Not To Be (Independent)

The following statement will make you want to find an easy chair, lie back in it, close your eyes, relax, and smile. The muscles in the back of your neck are going to ease up and your headache is going to disappear. Here it is: It is in the extremes of behavior and emotions that the stabilization of teen-agers is in progress. Don't you feel better already? The extremes that your teens display will help them become stable adults. Can you wait long enough for the transformation to take place? I hope so. But in the meantime, be prepared for some extreme mood changes.

Mood Checkup

One Day	Next Day
Sit on your lap	"Don't touch me!"
Talk	"Leave me alone."
Happy	"This day shouldn't have happened."
"I don't want to go."	"Why didn't you make me go?"
Pleased with self	"I'm so ugly."

These mood shifts occur because teens still need special support from their parents, and at the same time, they're trying to survive without that extra support. At this point you might want to make an amendment to the Beatitudes: "Blessed are the parents who are wise enough to want to understand their teens and, at the same time, do not resent what is happening and how it is happening."

If you make an effort to notice, you'll realize that your older teens have begun to master more of their environment by themselves. But if they cannot cope with something, secure teens usually will feel free to return to their parents for support. Turning to adults for advice doesn't mean that teens are regressing into dependency. They demonstrate their maturity by turning to others for help when they can't solve a problem alone.

It is difficult for teens and their parents to find a workable balance in the dependent-independent conflict. Sometimes I still tell my teens to get their proper rest, eat the right foods, not skip meals, or wear a cap during cold weather. After I finish my sermon, they smile at me, and I feel foolish. Then I know it's time for me to say, "I did this so much when you were small that I forget. Be patient with me. I'm trying."

I feel that dependence and independence can coexist. One can take precedence over the other as the need demands. I have not neglected my own activities in order to be free when my teens have felt dependent. I hope, however, that I have been available when their needs became overwhelming and that I've had time to give them the support that they needed from me.

Support comes in varied forms. I have held our teens' hands until they have fallen asleep. I have listened to them cry. I have suffered with them during their growing-up pains. I have tried to shelter them when it was proper to do so. As they have matured I have understood that they are finding their own ways of overcoming the growing pains.

I know that teens will eventually feel good about themselves, because I have seen this in the lives of our two older daughters. They will be able to stand alone and overcome obstacles that others put in their ways. They will live by the simple principle that God is interested in each phase of their lives.

Understanding this Declaration of Independence

I asked a mother what she thought about her teen becoming independent of her. She replied, "It doesn't matter what I think. I don't have any other alternatives, do I?" Even though you know there's no way to keep your teens from becoming independent, you'll still have questions about it.

But what will happen if parents ignore the development of independence? If we don't allow our teens to withdraw from us, they, as adults, may have to revert to the time when they were teen-agers. Through experimentation and decision-making, they will attain adulthood on their own. If they don't do this, they remain so dependent on their parents that they cannot function successfully without them. These parents cannot function without their teens. Both wind up being crippled.

Achieving independence is complicated because all human beings are basically selfish. That gives us the desire to hold on to what is no longer ours. This includes holding on to our teens when it's no longer right to do so. Fear is another reason why parents are reluctant to see their teens become independent. We're afraid that our teens will make wrong choices in their new freedom, because we still have vivid memories of some of our own wrong choices. These two factors could be why many of us make independence complicated.

One reason that teens break away is to develop an identity apart from their parents. They'll do things independent of their parents, and it'll take courage for them to do so. They still love their parents, but they don't have the total allegiance they once felt.

Let me give you an example. One of our daughters had a problem. We learned later that she felt that she had to work it out without involving us. All I understood at the time was that a fifteen-year-old was having a problem. I didn't know what it was, but I knew I was being asked to remove myself from the situation. My inclination was to say, "Tell me. I'll try to understand. Don't you need me just a little—as you used to?" That was the key: "You don't need me as you used to."

As a child, this same daughter would come crying to

me when she skinned her knee. I'd lift her up into my arms, wipe her tears, gently clean her wound, and promise her it would be all right. She believed me. I can draw a parallel from this. Even though she doesn't need me the way she once did, that doesn't mean she has stopped loving me. She has developed another kind of love that has grown out of respect for her parents who, in turn, respect her new independence from us. Her way of life has not been exactly like ours, but the foundations will always be there for her to rely on.

Take time to concentrate on your teens' independence from you. Weigh the pros and cons. You will begin looking at independence objectively. You'll begin to see positive outgrowths of it. You will probably admit that you wouldn't want it any other way.

I cannot see anything negative about teens becoming independent of their parents. It's the process by which it occurs that gives some of us trouble. But understanding what's going on can relieve us, to some extent, and give us the encouragement we need to be able to wait for the results.

The "How-to" of Independence

If you've read the first part of this chapter carefully, you've either reaffirmed what you already knew about independence or you're beginning to see the importance of it. Now that you have this in mind, I would like to give you examples of how some parents guided their teens into independence. I would also like to tell you where some of us went wrong.

Things Some Parents Did Right

A unique group of parents conceived the value of independence early in their children's lives. Their teens clean their rooms, earn their spending money, make their clothes, buy their own cars, and put themselves through college.

These parents evidently knew the full implications of handing out responsibilities at an early age. While most of us were admiring how cute and helpless our two-year-olds were, these parents were playing "Pick Up Toys" with their children. After their children learned the rules to that game, the parents began giving them other games to play. The chores corresponded to the ages and abilities of the children. The plan worked because everyone had well-defined responsibilities. The children were familiar with the game rules. They didn't know the game could be played any other way.

These children didn't always do their jobs perfectly, but they did them as well as they could. Bedspreads didn't always hang straight, kitchen counters were still a little sticky and greasy, and furniture wasn't too thoroughly dusted. But what would the children have learned about responsibilities if their parents had emphasized perfection instead of "your best"?

Things Some Parents Did Wrong

We shouldn't resent parents who knew the importance of assigning responsibilities early. Some of us knew that specific duties were important, but we didn't fully realize the place those duties would have in making our children independent. Other parents assigned themselves the title of law enforcement officers. Their demands were so great that their children felt defeated before they had had a chance to develop work skills.

Many of us did not work away from home when our children were small. It seemed natural for us to clean house, cook, wash, mend, and do whatever else was involved in a normal day. While we worked, the children played. We were not only performing our work well, but we were also doing tasks our children could have shared.

Later, we took a hard look at our children's endless energy, youthful strength, and endurance. Observation told us that their energy outlasted ours, their strength equaled ours, and their endurance left us exhausted.

However, a simple request that started with "would you mind" and ended with "carrying out the trash," "turning off the television," "answering the phone," "cleaning your room," "washing the car," or "mowing the lawn," would guarantee that teens were suddenly "tired" or "too busy" to help. These replies made us resent them. We saw them as lazy, indifferent, and insensitive to all we had to do. We couldn't, with clear consciences, blame them for their attitudes. They hadn't made work hard on us; we had made work hard on us. The situation looked bleak and unsolvable.

Through the years, many of us kept all the responsibilities to ourselves. We had not shared this particular aspect of "growing up" with our teens. During the time I was trying to put this idea of teen responsibilities in the right perspective, I earned, and also deserved, the nickname "Sally Sacrifice." Our daughters gave me that name because of my domestic martyrdom. Joan of Arc and Carrie Nation fought for special causes, but I was recognized for such heroic acts as sacrificing the last piece of dessert even though I wanted it, and eating the pieces of overly-done meat or the pieces that had the largest bones in them so that the others could enjoy the better pieces. I ran errands for the girls before I realized that their legs were stronger than mine. I stayed up late sewing for them when their stamina outlasted mine. I brought snacks to them from the kitchen when they were just as aware of its location as I was.

These were my choices. I said I enjoyed doing these things for them, and I still say it. However, I was not being fair to our children. My regret is that I decreased their independence by not allowing them to have responsibilities and by not giving them opportunities to do things for themselves. I was keeping them from becoming an active and necessary part of our family. Feeling needed is a basic human necessity. They didn't feel needed.

The girls needed responsibilities in our home, not only

because it helped us, but also because it would teach them that responsibility would be required in their school activities, their social obligations, and in their chosen vocations and marriages. If independence was an isolated factor, I might have seen its importance much sooner. But independence isn't isolated. It is only one of many facets that allows us to live successfully.

With which parents have you identified? If it's with the latter group, let me assure you that teens grow up in spite of their parents. I believe this, and I want you to believe it. Even parents who early on realized the importance of independence have made mistakes, and their teens will also grow up in spite of them.

The Starting Point

You can teach your teens to accept responsibility, although it won't be easy. Being aware that responsibility is necessary gets you ready at the goal line and makes you eager to win even if the odds of winning are stacked against you. It's exciting to work on existing situations in families, especially when you wonder how family members will respond. Before you begin, your family must see how unbalanced the responsibilities are.

TIME OUT

Sit down with your family. Appoint a secretary. Have the secretary put the names of each member across the top of a piece of paper.

List what each member is responsible for around the house. Read the lists aloud. Check the lists to see if anyone is carrying more of a load than he or she should.

Make a new list and shift the responsibilities to make a more balanced work force.

You also need to establish rules to assure that the assigned tasks are carried out. These rules will not always need to remain rigid. They will become more flexible as the teens get older, but in the beginning, rules are mandatory. For some reason, the word *rules* implies restrictions which intrude upon the teens' desires for freedom. Teens have a hard time accepting restrictions. They feel that some rules are unnecessary or out-of-date. They will question the rules about allowances, school involvement, socializing, curfews, dating, responsibilities for their rooms, and driving.

But teens and parents can work together to establish rules. The following Time Out may help.

TIME OUT

Give your teens reasons why certain rules are necessary.

Give them a chance to openly discuss rules that they agree or disagree with.

Decide what is accomplished by making certain rules.

Discuss which rules should be discarded, and why.

Decide what new rules should be made, and why.

Discuss which existing rules should be changed, and why.

Rules about two situations will be especially controversial. One of these situations is your teens' responsibilities for cleaning their rooms. To help set up the rules, ask your family to rate the appearance of your teens' rooms. Rate them from 1–10, 10 being the highest score. The cumulative score will give the teens an idea of how good or bad their rooms appear to others.

Most mothers cannot accept the way their teens choose to maintain their rooms. It doesn't bring any comfort for moms to hear other teens say, "You think this is messed up? You ought to see mine!" This doesn't keep mothers from being embarrassed when a long-time friend drops by to "see your house," all of it, your teen's room included.

You've used all the psychological methods—threats ("no allowance until . . ."), kindness, pleading, or embarrassment—to get them to clean their rooms. It doesn't help to know that other parents experience the same problems. When you've admitted defeat, don't find a dark corner and sit there groaning, "Why me?" Dig out your sense of humor, and when you've found it, run through the house, even through your teens' rooms, saying, "Someday, this shall pass away!" Then shut their doors.

If your teens understand that it's "their" room, "their" property, and "their" responsibility, where do you fit in? One mother offered this philosophy:

> I asked myself, "Is *my* room clean?" Then I make myself believe that there are more important things to be accomplished in this world than keeping a room straightened. If I try to get my teens to clean their rooms, am I doing it because I want to impress my friends, or to help keep me from looking bad?
>
> I don't believe some teens have time to keep their rooms straightened all the time because of the demands made on them at school. Just knowing they know how to clean their rooms is good enough for me. As long as they're doing well and accomplishing, that's more important than keeping their rooms clean all the time.

Maybe she's found the answer!

Another controversial set of rules are rules about using the car. Let's say that your teens have finished their driver's education class. They're ready to get their driving permits. It's time to sit down with your teens and define the rules for using the car. These include:

1. Their responsibilities (e.g., gas, cleaning, insurance)
2. The need to show respect for other family members who use the car
3. Consequences if the car is misused (and definition of "misused")
4. Guidelines as to where the car can and cannot be taken

Give a thorough explanation about insurance coverage and what procedures to follow in case of an accident. After discussing these things, ask your teens if any of these restrictions sound unreasonable. If they believe that some are not fair, discuss those rules until you come to some kind of agreement with each other. When everything is settled, hand them the car keys.

Some of you may not yet have teens who are old enough to drive. But you "veteran" parents will remember the first time you allowed your teens to drive you around town after they had gotten their driver's permits. You probably remember flinching when you thought they were getting too close to the parked cars, when you weren't sure they saw the yield signs, when they went over the center lines, or when they didn't apply the brakes as soon as you thought they should. Your right leg probably started getting stiff from excessive pressure to the floorboard, and the thought occurred to you that you were overdue to have your blood pressure checked.

Shortly after this, you gave them permission to drive the car alone. Remember this scene: You stand at the door watching them back out of the driveway. You hope they remember to look both ways before they get into the street. They're out of sight now. You move away from the door, wondering if the car insurance has been paid. You pray they'll get back safely. You have given them more responsibility, in addition to the advice you gave them before they left the house.

By the time you've finished wondering if you've told them everything, you hear the car horn signaling the message, "Look, Mom, I made it (without you)." They have learned to drive the car alone. They've proved to themselves, in one more way, that they can detach themselves from you—and it feels so good.

I believe teens want to be governed by fair rules. They want you to exert some authority pertaining to things that really matter. There will be protests. If these protests become more regular and stronger, discuss again why you and your teens established these guidelines. Protesting doesn't always mean teens disagree with the rules; they're just at odds with the restrictions placed upon them, even though they realize the rules are fair.

From Rules to Choices

When do teen-agers stop living by predetermined rules and begin living by their own choices? All of us are governed by the rules of nature; however, that doesn't necessarily mean that we are going to keep all of them. It doesn't take long to realize what will happen if we break some of nature's laws. But making choices isn't as clear-cut as abiding by rules. Choices carry the quality of uncertainty with them. Perhaps that is why we hesitate to place our teens in situations where they have to be completely responsible for their decisions.

Making choices is not new to your teens. You may not have been aware that you introduced decision-making to them early in their lives. Try to remember when you gave them the choice of whether they wanted:

> to eat peas or mashed potatoes,
> to play inside or outside,
> to have a friend over or to play alone,
> to wear a red shirt or a blue one,
> to get up on time or to be late for school.

As they got older they chose:

> to spend their allowances as soon as they received them or to save the money to buy something they really wanted,
>
> to study for a test and pass or not to study and fail,
>
> to drive properly and be safe or to drive recklessly and risk having an accident,
>
> to be responsible with a job and build a good reputation for future jobs or to be irresponsible and create a questionable reputation,
>
> to stay in control on a date and respect individual worth or to let emotions get out of control and risk life-changing consequences.

Notice that the second group of choices carries heavier responsibilities. You probably won't be around when your teens make most of these decisions. Since you won't be there, you no longer will be able to present the choices to your teens. Now, they're your teens' choices—their decisions. Making the decisions and living with the consequences are the complete responsibility of the decisions-maker.

Any kind of freedom carries restrictions with it; when our teens ignore these restrictions, various things are going to happen. I can remember telling a college professor that I was trying to explain to our daughters how certain wrong decisions could cause drastic changes in their lives. I explained this to my daughters so they wouldn't have to go through some of the same trying times I had experienced. The professor told me that was good, but asked, "Did you ever think that some of their learning is going to come through their mistakes?" He was right, but it's a truth hard for us to accept, even though we know its validity from our own experiences. Then what do we do when our teens make obvious mistakes? Do we step in and try to make things right, or do we blend into the background and convince ourselves that this mistake will help them make better choices in the future?

Rules Versus Choices

When do we give our teens complete freedom of choice? I believe that common sense is sometimes our only measuring stick. Being "reasonably" permissive with our teens requires the greatest wisdom of all.

It was difficult for my husband and me to decide when complete freedom of choice should begin. We decided to gradually give our daughters an increasing freedom of choice through the teen years. By the beginning of their senior year in high school they had complete freedom of choice. By allowing them to make their own choices at this time, we were close enough to give them support and offer guidance. During this time I had to muster up all the faith I had ever reserved and activate the trust I said I had in our daughters.

Our college-age daughters have had enough insight to recognize some of their classmates and roommates were not given opportunities to make their own choices while they were still living at home. In college, the need to make decisions was suddenly thrust upon them and they had difficulties making choices.

Teens won't handle every situation perfectly, either. The difference between us and our teens is that we've had more years to make more mistakes.

One of our daughters told me that she had to leave the house to think about a decision she had to make. When she came home, she didn't hesitate to tell me that she had walked around aimlessly, had become tired, and had gone into a hotel lobby to sleep. I wanted to close my eyes to the hurt that she was experiencing. It didn't occur to me to be concerned with what other people might have thought when they saw her sleeping in the hotel lobby; I was too concerned about her and how she had tried to solve her problems.

We may believe that she chose an unusual way to reach her decision. It may be that we wouldn't have worked it out that way, but if we would have told her how to do it, it wouldn't have been her choice. In the past few years, this same young woman has had to make several big decisions, and she has done beautiful jobs with them. I believe that her success has been an outgrowth of her parents allowing her to flounder with smaller decisions. The potential for success was always there, even though it didn't always seem to be.

I don't know what determines when a mistake is not a mistake. A decision may appear to be a mistake, but in the long run, may turn out to be a lasting lesson for our teens. Remember, mistakes are inevitable in acquiring independence.

It bothers us to see our teens make wrong decisions. However, most of their wrong moves will not end tragically. At the same time, we must be aware that a few of their wrong decisions could negatively alter their dreams. Sometimes it's good for teens to hear their parents talk about some of the mistakes they made as teen-agers and what they learned through those mistakes. I have coined a new proverb: "A teen who findeth parents who will admit to some of their mistakes, findeth a good thing."

Some parents know precisely when to be "reasonably" permissive. Let me share this story with you. A teen-ager let it be known that he resented any authority. When he was eighteen years old, he decided that he was not going to submit to authority any longer. He quit school and got a job with a singing group. After he had had the job for two weeks, he decided he didn't want it as much as he had thought he did. He went home, worked all summer, and entered college in the fall. Can you imagine how hard his first decision was for his parents to accept? You may have categorized the parents' acceptance of their son's decision to quit school as an unwise judgment on the parents' part. I feel that they had the wisdom to tell the boy that there would always be things he'd have to figure out for himself and that he'd have to carry the full responsibility for his decisions. It wouldn't have been wise for them to have disagreed with his strategy because what he did was right for him.

Freedom of choice must be gradual. Parents don't allow a junior-high child to have the same freedom of choices as they allow a senior in high school. The teens must have some guidance in their choices at first. The older they become, the more choices they should have. If the choices are big ones, mark some perimeters and encourage your teens to operate within them. Even then, they may try to flex their wills against yours.

None of us want to harm our teens by not allowing them to develop their own way of life, nor do we want to keep them from being the persons they were made to be. The members of each family must decide when parents should start loosening their grasp on their teens and how they're going to do it.

During one of those questionable times, I thought it would help for me to call a friend who is a family counselor. When I called him, my throat was tight, my voice was pitched an octave higher than usual, and my hands were clammy. I explained the problem. He advised, "Hang loose. You've got to hang loose!" I thought, "That's easy for you to say. I want you to call me when you have a teen, and I'll give you the same advice. Then you'll see how easy it is to 'hang loose!'"

Teens have to struggle in order to see where they stand, what they value, and what they feel is important. I hear older teens saying to their parents, "Thanks for standing behind me in my decisions, for believing in me, and for trusting me." With this statement, your teens are trying to let you know how they appreciate your confidence in them. By placing your confidence in them, you're showing that you respect their desires to become their own persons. You're allowing them to gradually be set free.

"Do I Have to Go to Church?"

Parents don't want—and aren't prepared—to hear this question. The reluctance to go to church is one more apparent change that we might need to accept. Sometimes this question takes a more subtle form. Here's how one of our daughters chose to express her desire to make her own decisions concerning church attendance.

Every Sunday, as the time approached for youth choir practice at church, our daughter created all kinds of excuses not to go. She usually lost the battle (or were we losing the battle?) when we insisted that she go. Finally, her persistence outlasted ours. I thought, "What's the use? I'm tired of fighting her. If the idea of going to church had never been invented she wouldn't have been more pleased."

After youth choir practice came the evening worship services. I thought it made matters doubly worse that her dad was the minister, and she wasn't even showing up for these services. The conflict resulted in our leaving the house each Sunday evening angry with one another, and leaving behind a teen-ager with a deep sense of guilt. It was a dreadful time for us until my husband and I thought about our daughter's personality. She had never liked being in front of a crowd. This became even more evident when she entered the teen years. In school, she always volunteered to help with makeup or stage scenery for all the drama productions. She was helpful and good at what she did; nevertheless, she was always behind the scenes. She felt conspicuous in youth choir because it performed before the congregation during each evening worship service. We believed that all youth, including our daughter, liked music and should be in the choir. It was a false assumption.

We had to make ourselves realize that some of her disinterest was because of her personality. When we realized this, it became easier for us to leave her at home on Sunday evenings. Our only stipulation was that she couldn't go anywhere else during that time. She didn't seem to resent the restriction. I stopped being angry with her, and I believe that she no longer felt guilty for not attending church with us.

It was at this same time that she asked me to stop singing in the adult choir on Sunday morning so that she and I could sit together. I loved singing in the choir, but I loved my daughter more. I explained her request to the choir director. He understood my concern and stood by my decision to drop out of choir temporarily. My daughter and I have never mentioned this time we had together during the worship services, but I've never regretted my decision.

Teens have a multitude of reasons for seemingly rejecting religion, or at least part of it. I respect teens' right to question established ways of the church and to wonder if some of the manmade practices are of lasting value. Have you ever been put to sleep by someone using a monotone voice and giving a dissertation on the wanderings of the twelve tribes of Israel, or by someone trying to explain, in one hour, his theories of the symbols used in the Book of Revelation?

I'm not so liberal that I can't see value in our teens being active in the organized church. I do not believe that they are rejecting the teachings of the church; they just don't accept everything that the church is offering. I feel that this is another area of questioning in their lives. During some of these times, parents may also question the value of many church practices and programs, but they don't dare to admit it. I believe our teens are trying to decide if there really is substance in spiritual teachings and whether those teachings really work.

Parents need this, also. They need to ask, "Is my faith vital to my life? Is it a living faith through the week or does it surface only on Sunday? Do I react in a Christ-like manner in all the things that happen behind our closed doors of home? Do I display Christian virtues in my business? Can my children see Christ living through me?"

No one can say that all teens will, at some point, reject the church. However, I feel we must give our teens room to doubt when they no longer want to engage in any part of the activities the church offers. If your faith is a genuine faith, it will be contagious to your teens. A mother was working with a group of teens in her church, even though her daughter had chosen to stop going to that particular youth group. The mother said, "I can reach other teens, but I can't reach my own daughter." Several years later, the mother found out that her daughter had learned many things by listening and watching her prepare various youth activities. The daughter was learning, although she was not actively participating with the other youth.

I do not believe in coercing older teens to attend church. Force can have an adverse effect in later years. If there is a hint of rejection now that isn't allowed to express itself, it could present itself more strongly later on. One young married woman feels very definitely that her husband was not allowed to express just how deeply he "hated" going to church as a teen-ager. Today she says, "He's going through a silent rebellion. I only hope he'll get it straightened out before our children get much older."

TIME OUT

If you're receiving verbal or nonverbal messages from your teens that they're becoming disinterested in church, discuss the matter as soon as you detect their disinterest. Try to find out what they don't like and why they don't like it. Some of their reasoning may seem unjustified, but it makes sense to them.

Decide together what they feel would be fair to them

at this time. Don't expect them to give the answers you want them to give.

We need to do our spiritual homework with our children during the early years of their lives. If and when this outward rebellion presents itself later, we can hold firmly to this promise: "Train up a child in the way he should go; and when he is old he will not depart from it" (Prov. 22:6, KJV). Read II Timothy 3:15 for further encouragement.

I can recount only a small portion of our daughter's spiritual rebellion and subsequent spiritual growth. When she was in college, she sometimes was alone, and all she had to strengthen and encourage her were her talks with God and her belief in Him. He led her gently through those days. He led her to love a young man who was not a Christian, and in turn, she led him to love God personally as she did. Her spiritual struggles are not over. Mine aren't either, but I refer you to another command: all of us are to "grow in spiritual strength and become better acquainted with our Lord and Savior Jesus Christ" (II Peter 3:18, LB). I am eternally grateful that God intervened and kept us from destroying this fragile part of our daughter's life.

Sorting Out

I wrote a letter to our youngest daughter shortly after she had left home for college. I wish I would have written it to her sooner, but maybe she wouldn't have been ready to receive it then. In the letter I mentioned how teenagers have so many choices to make and how I admire the way many of them stick by their decisions. Here's a portion of the letter:

Remember when I used to ask you to sort clothes on wash day? You would put the white clothes in one pile, towels in another pile, and colored clothes in another pile. You knew what piles most of the clothes belonged in, but there were some things that weren't really dark and some things that had both white and dark colors in them. They didn't seem to fit in any pile.

(The sermon) There are some things that will always belong in your life. You know where they go. You have them in the right perspective. There are other things you're not quite sure where they belong, and still other things that don't belong anywhere in your life.

When you weren't sure where those questionable clothes went, you'd ask me, and I would tell you where they'd work best.

You're going to be doing lots of sorting out these next few years. I'm glad you don't have to make these decisions by yourself. Anytime you're not sure about something, simply ask God to help you. Ask Him where things belong in your life. Ask Him to reveal to you whether they should even be a part of your life. You can depend on Him because He said all you have to do is ask.

We all give our children rules by which to live. The time comes when our rules for life must turn into their choices for living. Teens will have to handle many things on their own. They're going to develop a sense of maturity, and along with it, a sense of responsibility. In this maturing, they will establish new relationships with us. They can't hold onto the dependence which they had as children, although they will recall the force of those earlier experiences in the parent/child relationship.

None of us will ever forget the day our children took their first steps alone. We used every trick we could devise to get them to walk to us. Then, as they grew up, as they felt freer to make their own decisions, as they accepted full responsibility for those decisions, we had to admit that instead of walking toward us, they were walking away from us. They had been doing this gradually all through their lives. At this point, they're no longer completely dependent on us. We aren't around to hold their hands and steady their steps. We must rejoice in the directions their lives are taking them, just as we rejoiced over their first steps alone.

I now have two daughters in their twenties who have developed into totally independent people. I've wondered how they've been able to get by so well without me around! But it happens, even if you're not ready for it. I've dared to survive so I can tell you about the beauty of children becoming independent of their parents. Don't you believe the parents who say, "It gets worse as they get older!" It isn't true. The new relationship you form with your teens has to be one of the most satisfying relationships of your life.

Make independence available to your teens. Graciously hand it to them, and they'll take the parts that they feel they're ready to handle. Intermingled with their desire for freedom will still be a need for your support.

"Just Look at These Legs"

When one of our daughters was in the seventh grade, she rarely missed a day of standing on the rim of the bathtub—her eyes transfixed on the mirror across the room—saying disgustedly, "Just look at these legs!" I lost count of the times I tried to explain to her that her legs would eventually fill out. In her opinion, the size and shape of her legs would never change. She would be a marked woman for life because of her thin legs.

All of us have changes to cope with, but the changes teens go through are magnified because they are so drastic and rapid. Physical and social changes invade their childhood securities, and they don't like it. What they're seeing and feeling is totally different from anything they've experienced until now, and it's happening without their consent. During this time their self-image is probably at its lowest point.

Society makes self-acceptance extremely difficult for our teens, and for some, impossible. Commercials imply that to be anybody, you must have sex appeal, a toothy smile, and a well-proportioned body. To be beautiful or handsome (what is beautiful or handsome?), women must be thin (when are they too heavy?); men, muscular (how muscular?). You must be aware of and possess the latest fashions in clothing (who wears most of those latest fashions except the professional models?). You must get a college degree (why?), and you must be accepted and be seen with the right group of people (who can say who the right group is?).

When our teens look down and see partially-developed bodies, smile and see braces instead of teeth, fall over things that aren't there, it is hard for them to realize that there is a specific place for them in society. Physical changes and social acceptance seem to take forever. The boys want instant muscles, beards, and girlfriends. The girls want instant curves and boyfriends.

Parents must recognize and understand the self-image which our teens develop during this crucial time may be the picture of their individual worth which they will carry with them the rest of their lives. We don't have the ability to pass on a healthy self-concept through genes; it is learned, and we have to help our teens learn it. I firmly believe that it is within the family that self-worth is established. Although teens' self-worth will be continually modified throughout their lifetimes, it is most vulnerable during the teen years.

How do we foster positive ideas in our teens' minds? How do we let them know that it isn't mandatory that they look like other people, act like them, or accomplish the same things in the same ways as others do? Our teens are unique. Because they are, they are not going to look like other people. And their accomplishments will differ. But they don't like the word *unique* because it denotes being different from the crowd, and they are allergic to being different. They won't always be opposed to their uniqueness, but now they are. They want to blend in, not to stand out.

All of us have to find our own effective ways of gradually letting our teens know that there are no other people in this world exactly like them. They're going to be able to do things with their lives that no one else will be able to do. Most of the time, they'll detect what you're trying to do, and they'll remark, "You're just saying that because you're my mom." But you know how important self-acceptance is; therefore, you will want to work diligently to instill it in your teens.

How did we establish and nurture a healthy self-image? None of us acquired it automatically; we could see only our faults. I believe the word *gawky* comes close to describing how I felt about myself when I was a teen. My coordination was poor. I fell down a lot. The glass of water that spilled was usually mine. Many times I would cry myself to sleep because I thought no one liked me the way I was. I wondered why there were no boys taller than I was, and I'm sure they wondered why girls grew faster than boys. I didn't like my skinny arms, and my friend hated her big arms. I'd shop for a new dress and look in the mirror to see a dress waistline four inches above my natural waistline. It was hard for me to accept what I saw. I hated my body for not being able to fit into any dress.

I didn't like myself most of the time, but there were three people who did—my family. They didn't—and probably still don't—know how deeply I resented myself during those years. However, of all the doubts I ever had about myself, I never doubted their love for me. It surpassed any negative thought I had about myself. It was their steady, daily love for me that was to carry over into the remaining years of my life. I cannot overemphasize how necessary this support was during my teen years.

The other thing I received from them, which was an outgrowth of their love, was their acceptance of me. They accepted the way I looked and what I was trying to work out in my life, but they didn't expect more of me than I was capable of giving. Their attitudes toward me did not waver. Because my family accepted me, it was much easier for me to begin to accept myself. I began seeing my worth, not only through their eyes, but also through mine. Because these two factors—love and acceptance—had meant so much to me, I was determined that our teens were going to experience these same positive influences in their lives.

"Infirmities" of Teens

A teen-ager had been combing his hair for a long time. His family was waiting for him to come to breakfast. He finally appeared, looking extremely unhappy. He sat down and said, "You know, some mornings I just wake up ugly." If you asked every teen-ager, "What are you most self-conscious about?" most of them would probably answer,"My body!" Somewhere within the gradual process of finding self-worth, our teens must learn to accept their physical appearances. This becomes the prerequisite for successfully achieving a mature personal identity.

Teens begin examining their changing bodies. Intellectually, they know that they will change physically during the teen years, but they don't realize how these changes will affect them while they're experiencing them. Since there are absolutely no set patterns for the way these teens will develop, they will have no way of knowing how fast or how slowly their development will take place. In their minds, they envision the finished product, and if it's any less than what they've dreamed, they become highly critical of themselves. You may get blamed for the finished product because of the physical characteristics they've inherited from you. You'll be accused of passing on short fingers, toes, and eyelashes; weak backs, ankles, and knees; big hips, ears, noses, feet, and stomachs; bad complexions, freckles, and moles; frizzy hair, and knobby knees. (One teen complained, "My knees look like tomatoes.")

Girls don't want to be too tall, and boys don't want to be too short. They learn what the average height is for men and women, and they want to be within an inch of that. Their height concerns them because girls are supposed to be shorter than boys, and boys are supposed to be taller than girls. Why? Society says! In an effort to cooperate with society, tall girls subtract an inch off their height when they are asked how tall they are, and short boys automatically add at least two inches onto their height. Tall girls seem more self-conscious around short girls (who are wishing they were taller), and the short boys are looking for other boys their height so they won't feel conspicuous. One tall teen put an end to a question that was asked her almost daily: "How's the weather up there?" She spit on one questioner and said, "It's raining." As drastic as this seems, most teens are trying to conjure up answers that will leave such a lasting impression on the questioner that the questions won't be asked again.

Teens who are less than average height become equally frustrated. They get nicknames that are just as humiliating as the nicknames tall teens get. Short teens are asked, "How short are you, anyway?" or, "Aren't you ever going to get any taller?" These questions are painful and unnecessary for teens to answer.

The question of size is as vital as the question of height. Overweight teens, especially girls, will try any kind of diet that insures "weight loss as you wait." They'll try the eighteen-day water diet, the three-grapefruits-a-day diet, the two-pounds-of-cottage-cheese-a-day diet, or dieting by starvation. Parents are the ones who have to watch their teens wither away before their eyes. There is no game, reward, or threat great enough to make these teens eat. Another group of teens will want to eat all the time. They won't be able to gain weight, so eating becomes an obsession with them. You'll prepare three well-balanced meals each day. They'll eat the meals, and eat before and after them. Some days you will wish that they would at least wait until you had the dishes cleared from the table before they start looking for something else to eat.

Foot size can be another source of irritation to your teens. It's humiliating for teens to be directed to the children's shoe department in order to find shoes that will fit them. It's equally awkward for teens to force their feet into size-eight shoes when they've been measured for a size ten.

If your teens are growing rapidly, it's natural that they're going to have poor coordination. When children sit down at a table, it's considered a simple motion. For these same individuals turned teens, sitting down can mean disaster, chaos, ruin. Teens often get yelled at a lot for kicking chairs unintentionally. This clumsiness has to do with the new size of their feet and their new leg length. They don't mean to cause disruptions; those disruptions just happen.

Even skin color and hair texture cause teens dissatisfaction. As one teen said, "My skin is terminally white." These teens will want to have dark tans. You will have no way of weighing or registering the layers of skin that you'll doctor and that these fair-skinned teens will lose to annual sunburns. The dark-skinned teens will want to be darker, and they will become dedicated sun worshipers. Teens with straight hair will want curly hair. Curly-haired teens will iron their hair, press it between encyclopedias, wear weights on the ends of it, or rub any mixture into their hair that says it will induce straightness. Girls have specific grievances about their breast development. If the current fashion trend deemphasizes the large bustline, the flat-chested girls become more comfortable with their underdeveloped breasts. If fashion says they must have a large bustline, there is a dilemma for girls with small busts. Girls with large busts have other problems. There aren't many ways these girls can conceal their size, and it's traumatic for them when boys start making lewd remarks.

During these years, boys begin trying to find excuses to shave, and girls begin the lifelong process of shaving their legs. Boys and girls hate their knockknees or their "too long" chins. They wear hair styles that cover as much of their faces as possible, yet allow for appropriate vision. They want to trade their hair, arms, feet, fingers, dimples, or freckles with anyone who has the opposite characteristics. They'll ask if they can have plastic surgery on the physical features that they feel they can't possibly live with for the rest of their lives. This should be enough to show us how desperate they are about their appearances.

"Infirmities" Changed to "Assets"

It's interesting (or is it frustrating?) to observe how extremely critical teens become about their personal appearances. We can accept the changes they're going through more lightly than they can because we know that in all probability they'll be pleased with the results. Some of the things they feel most negative about now may turn out to be their greatest assets.

The following Time Outs can help make you aware of your teens' problems. Parents also need to participate in these Time Outs. In sharing the results, your teens will begin to see that adults also have physical improvements they want to make.

TIME OUT

Ask each family member to draw an outline of his body as he sees it. He is to put an "X" on the parts he doesn't like.

Ask who would like to reveal his dislikes first.

Discuss what parts can be corrected by diet, exercise, makeup, or a different hair style.

If some things can't be changed—height, foot size, skin color—introduce the idea that some things in life are unchangeable. They are to be accepted or camouflaged, and lived with.

ALTERNATE TIME OUT

Ask your teens, "What are the things about your physical appearance that you don't like and that could be changed?"

"What would you be willing to do to change them?"

"Which things are necessary to accept and how can you accept them successfully?"

Many times changes will include additional expenses. Teens may have to help with the finances. If teens want to wear contact lenses, they might be more responsible for the care of the lenses if they help with the purchase.

The same is true with braces for their teeth. Many families can afford this expense, but just as many families can't. Perfectly straight teeth do not guarantee a beautiful smile, but some teens feel that straight teeth are a prerequisite for any smile. So if you are one of the families who can't bear the full expense of braces, encourage motivated teens to find jobs which will allow them to help defray the expense.

When things start appearing on teens' faces that have never been present before, they may become uneasy about themselves. Freckles, sunburns, and scratches were never taken seriously before, but now pimples and other blemishes become catastrophes. Teens will tell you that their faces stay clear until some special event is about to take place; then their faces are bombarded with unwanted blemishes. These occur because a chemical imbalance overstimulates the oil glands of the skin. Getting upset can also cause a pimple attack.

Few teens can get through these years without some kind of complexion problem. Your teens may need only to cleanse their faces thoroughly and regularly, follow a proper diet, and drink sufficient water. Or they may have to secure the services of a competent dermatologist.

Many times these doctors will suggest that when girls start using makeup they should consider a nonallergenic brand. When teens begin feeling good about their faces, many of their other problems will also be minimized.

Many boys, especially those interested in sports, desire larger muscles. They will exercise, run several miles a day, eat high-protein diets, and work out diligently with weights. The effort to build up their muscles will pay off by enabling them to perform more skillfully. It will also help them gain social recognition and acceptance. In most cases, it will help to attract the opposite sex. Many of these boys will want their own weights with which to work out. If their interest is great enough they will find ways to purchase their own weights. If money is a problem, encourage them to take advantage of those available at school or civic recreation centers.

Another change girls start to notice is the widening of their hips. If their hips measure more than thirty-two inches, they believe they're entirely too large, and they want to get rid of whatever they consider excess. If they don't like the idea of going on a watercress diet, they might want to consider regular jogging or brisk walking. These two exercises are particularly good for the hips and thighs and are sure-fire slimming activities. Tell your teens to give it a month's try. If they will do it, they will be pleased with the results. A two-mile jog or walk will do two things: improve their mental outlook and get their bodies into shape. If they don't like to jog or walk alone, volunteer to join them. Until you've tried it, you can't know the lasting benefits—all of them good.

If your teens have severe weight problems, you may want to consult a physician who can recommend a diet to help your teens lose weight properly. If you also have a weight problem, you may want to join your teens in the diet. Many other teens have trouble gaining weight. You may also want to talk with a physician to see what foods will help these teens to gain weight.

When your daughters show signs of breast development, visit a store with a clerk who can help fit them properly with a bra. Well-fitted bras help girls feel more comfortable. Avoid clothing that might overemphasize a small bustline. For the girls with large busts, there are styles of clothing that can draw attention away from their bustlines.

Clothing styles, colors, and even fabrics can correct many physical features. Thin, tall teens should be encouraged to steer away from short sleeves, tight-fitting clothing, certain types of shorts and bathing suits, or anything that would draw attention to their physiques. Choosing simple, tailored fashion lines for overweight teens can provide an effective disguise for their weight.

Boys are as self-conscious about their hair as girls. Beauticians who keep up to date on the new trends can help eliminate stubborn hair. The simple solution to "I can't get my hair to do anything" may be proper cutting and styling. Choosing a good shampoo and conditioner may achieve satisfying results.

When your teens feel more secure with their biological makeup, they may find it somewhat easier to accept the parts that can't be changed. Hereditary traits must be considered and accepted.

When you finally hear still small voices, and they're your teens' giving themselves compliments such as, "Hey, I don't look half bad, do I?" or "I like the way I look—now!" you know that their respect for self is about to make its debut.

The Group Troops

It is essential for teens to start feeling good about their personal appearances. This is preliminary to gaining a healthy self-concept. This process wouldn't be nearly as complicated if another equally important element didn't start showing up at the same time. Not only are our teens becoming concerned with their physical changes, but simultaneously they want to be recognized and accepted socially. They have to find ways of connecting their lives successfully with other people's lives. They want to share what they know they have to offer to others, if others will only give them a chance. They want to achieve satisfying social acceptance, at least to a degree that will help them know that they're worth something.

It is evident how badly they want to be a part of a group. They may try to develop certain habits in order to be accepted by a group. Why do they do this? "Everybody needs to feel that somebody (preferably a lot of some-bodies) likes him because he's likable. Everybody needs to belong to some body—by free choice."[1] These groups will allow your teens an outlet for healthy rebellion. They will support your teens in their ideas and actions, which won't always agree with yours. When your teens walk out the door, two groups will influence them more than you do. These two groups will either help your teens build positively onto their growing self-esteem, or they will re-strict your teens in such a way that they will seriously question whether they are of any value at all.

The group that will be the most decisive factor in your teens' search for worth will be their peers. I don't know how popular peer groups get started, but it is extremely important to your teens that they belong to one of them. It may be more difficult than your teens ever dreamed it would be to break into one of these groups. It's painful enough for parents, but there is no pain equal to that which teen-agers suffer when they want to belong to a particular group and are excluded. The pain begins when they're left out of a group because of physical appearance, social standing, religious difference, moral values, na-tionality, or personality traits. They may be blackballed because of their fathers' vocations, the location of their

1. Dorothy and T. Garvice Murphree, *Understanding Youth* (Nash-ville: Convention Press, 1969).

homes, or the family income. It isn't fair, but that's the way the social system works. The type of peer group your teens become identified with will influence their concept of self-worth for the rest of their lives. Peer groups can be divided into three basic categories.

The first category includes teens with the outgoing personalities. They're naturally friendly, well-liked, competitive achievers. They hold class offices. They're sharp dressers. They're the ones who are recommended to represent their school on numerous occasions. They are cheerleaders, date the football captains, are elected homecoming queens, become beauty pageant contestants, are student-council members, superstars of the sports department, first-chair trumpet players, leads in the school plays, or number-one debaters.

The next category consists of the quiet, consistent achievers. They make good grades, but may not get on the honor roll. Their names will probably never appear in the school or town newspaper. They're in sports, but they're not the starters. They miss getting an excellent rating at a music or debate contest by one point. They help with elections, but they don't run for office. They are the makeup, stage, and scenery managers for the plays, but they're never center stage and never are applauded. They're the ones who sing well but never sing solos. They're not recognized as the hometown Top Ten. They dress well but wear bargains or clothes made by Mom.

The third category is not actually recognized as a group. They're "the gang." They're the underachievers, the irresponsibles, the unrecognizables, the drifters, the ones who "couldn't care less." Or are they? I believe that this is the group that is silently crying out, "Please, someone, tell me I'm worth something."

The second special group of people who are influential in your teens' developing self-worth is their teachers. They're the ones who should have the wisdom of Solomon, the insight of Socrates, the patience of Job, and the compassion of Jesus. They should be required to take a test to see if they are competent to handle the task of influencing teens positively during this time of developing self-worth.

It's never the majority of people, but the minority, who keep gray clouds hanging over one's opinion of self. Teachers are no exceptions. The teachers who "hit it off" with teens find it easy to identify with them and draw them out. However, the teachers whose personalities conflict with teens can have adverse effects and sometimes lifelong negative results. Boys who are highly skilled in sports will catch the eye of the coach, while the other boys will fade into the grass on the ballfield. Music teachers may distinctly hear the solo voices but will not be tuned in to the voices that blend. The teachers who recognize students with Einstein minds may neglect the teens who are still using their fingers to add and subtract.

None of us parents can find a price tag big enough to pin on teachers who see the potential of each student in their classes. These teachers are the chosen few who will be instrumental in helping our teens discover their self-worth. Their time with our teens will not be over when the dismissal bell rings. They will never consider the extra time they spend with their students an invasion of their personal time. By the way they teach, treat, and speak to our teens, they're saying, "You're going to make it because I believe in you." It's this idea of "believing in" that gives teens a glimmer of what self-esteem can do in their lives.

I am not implying that teens with leadership abilities shouldn't be recognized and be allowed to develop their abilities. I'm not saying it isn't good for teens to be recognized for their accomplishments. I *am* saying that if a good self-concept is so important for everyone, why can't we recognize the accomplishments of the second and third categories? How can the order of the universe be changed to let the majority of teens feel that their successes, no matter how small or insignificant, are just as important as those of the first category?

Even though your teens' peers and teachers are competing for most of your teens' time and influencing them significantly, you're still not completely off the ballfield. You are still your teens' private pep and fan club. You'll watch them from the sidelines, and you'll know when you're being called in to help complete an important play. You'll believe in your teens when no one else will or when they momentarily stop believing in themselves. You can do this because you can see their intrinsic worth long before it is firmly established.

The following Time Outs will give you and your family an idea of how your teens feel about themselves.

TIME OUT

Ask family members to name something they achieved before they were ten years old, then between ten and fifteen years old, then older.

If there are younger children participating, ask them to mention some things they've done this past week that they've been pleased with.

Notice: If your teens have a hard time thinking of anything, it might indicate that they have poor self-concepts. Encourage them by telling them some of the things you've noticed about them. They may be thinking only in terms of things that have received public recognition.

TIME OUT

Give each person a chance to complete this statement: "Right now I feel _____ about myself." Whether the statement is negative or positive, discuss those feelings with each other.

The "Ayes" Have It

Parents can go two different routes to help teens develop a positive self-image. The first route never works, but families try it anyway. Consider these scenes.

> Teen cleans kitchen. Dad's reaction: "Why didn't you clean the living room, too?"

> Teen struggles with hemming a dress. Shows her mother. Mother's comment: "That's okay, but it's awfully crooked, isn't it?"

> Teen shows parents his "B" grade on a test. Dad says: "Uh-huh, but next time, why don't you try for an 'A'?"

Scene changes.

> Dad brings home paycheck. Family implies: "Why don't you get a better job so we won't have to skimp so much?"

> Mom spends the afternoon preparing an exotic meal. Family members comment: "It tastes pretty good, but next time why don't you fix . . . ?"

Sometimes we joke with each other in a negative way, but just as many times, we don't joke. With our verbal hammers, we pound each family member further down until all that is left exposed is a painfully low self-image. Some parents still wonder if "I'm good for anything." This attitude is bound to carry over into their teens' lives. It takes awhile to discipline the mind to grasp the idea of good self-esteem.

These Time Outs may help you to evaluate your idea of your self-worth. When these suggestions become steady influences on you, you will want to share them with your teens.

TIME OUT

Find a place to be alone. Complete this sentence, "I'm good at _____." Be frank with yourself as you evaluate your strengths. You may embarrass yourself even though you're alone, because you have never boasted about yourself before.

Maybe you can fry an egg without breaking the yolk, keep the mending caught up, grow a lovely garden, make your house attractive, or share a cup of coffee at just the right time with a friend. Even if things don't seem significant and you think some things aren't worth mentioning, mention them.

This next Time Out is best of all—one you must pass on to your teens when you begin to see how it affects your life.

TIME OUT

Every time (and it has to be every time if you want to see some results) you have a negative thought about yourself, replace it with a positive thought about yourself.

Most of us are generous at selling ourselves short, so it isn't difficult to think of our negative points. It is much more difficult to come up with positive thoughts, since we haven't trained our minds to think positively. The value of accenting the positives in your life and eliminating the negatives is implied in this Scripture, "For as he thinketh in his heart, so is he" (Prov. 23:7, KJV).

Teens hear "put-downs" at school from their peers, teachers, and other insensitive adults. They don't need to hear them from their parents, too. They feel badly enough about themselves without their parents throwing more darts at them. If you have a choice of being a negative or a positive influence on your teens, isn't it logical to choose the positive way?

There are numerous ways parents can help their teens feel good about themselves. If you've spent hours giving out negatives and getting negatives back, start taking a more positive approach with your teens. Maybe you aren't as sensitive as you should be about the need people have for developing a healthy attitude toward themselves. Think about the people who have influenced you the most. They are usually the ones who believed in you and made you feel that you were someone special.

For starters, think about some of the things your teens do that you don't like. They're never ready on time. They complain when you ask them to help around the house. It takes them forever to get out of bed each morning. They don't come home when they're supposed to. They date the wrong people. They're always going to do things "later." They never clean out the shower . . . and on and on.

Now focus on their strengths: their kindness to children and to older people, their concern for their friends, their empathy for those who are suffering. Consider the way they do certain things without complaining, volunteer to help around the house, show their appreciation for the things you do for them, spontaneously say "thank you," value other peoples' feelings, write notes to share thoughts they find hard to say, are attentive during parent-teen lectures that weren't necessary, and laugh at jokes you've told over and over.

As you witness these strengths, don't hesitate to tell

your teens about them. Praise your teens. One word of caution, though: don't tell them all of their attributes at once, or they may suspect that you have an ulterior motive. Use these Time Outs to help family members learn to praise each other.

TIME OUT

Ask each family member to tell something he appreciates about another family member, or ask, "What can you say to another family member to help him feel better about himself?"

TIME OUT

Encourage each person to respond to the following statements, verbally or on paper.
1) The kind of person I think I am.
2) The kind of person others think I am.
3) The kind of person I would like to become.

TIME OUT

During the week, find ways to encourage your teens. Notice how you encourage them and how they respond after you encourage them.

These are introductory steps for building a good self-image. If your family comes up short in the area of handing out genuine compliments to each other, it may be up to you to set the pace for making this a regular practice within your home. At first your teens will probably say, "Aw, Mom," but take it to mean, "Thanks for noticing."

"I Like Myself . . . Now!"

A senior-high girl said, as she watched a junior-high group being dismissed from classes, "No one should ever have to be that age. I can remember those years, and it didn't seem like me. That's weird. I didn't like myself."

Helping teens love themselves is essential. This is the ingredient that will help them survive. If we can help them love themselves, several things will follow. They will start nurturing themselves, protecting themselves, admitting their failures, encouraging themselves, and praying for themselves. When this hurdle is cleared we need to start making a slow exit from their lives. We won't be able to evaluate how we've helped our teens because our consistent efforts may not show results for several years. They will have to want to recognize their worth and understand that with that recognition must come some years of struggle. That's the part we don't like, but we can keep in mind that this struggling will become less severe as they begin distinguishing themselves from others. They will begin to see that it isn't necessary to be like other people and they won't want to be like other people. They'll learn that everyone has his or her own set of strengths and weaknesses. This revelation will help them to accept themselves more readily. They will have come a long way since they started their search for self-worth.

From:
   "I'm a big fat zero."

To:
   "I've got more going for me than I thought I did."

   "No matter what you say or do to me, I'm still a person of worth."

   "I have the power within me to do anything that needs to be done."

Everyone needs to feel he or she has intrinsic worth. Teens need this more than adults do. If there are times when they won't allow you to let them know just how special they are, refer them to these verses.

[God], you made all the delicate, inner parts of my body, and knit them together in my mother's womb. Thank you for making me so wonderfully complex! It is amazing to think about. Your workmanship is marvelous—and how well I know it. You were there while I was being formed in utter seclusion! You saw me before I was born and scheduled each day of my life before I began to breathe. Every day was recorded in your Book! How precious it is, Lord, to realize that you are thinking about me constantly! (Psalm 139:13–17a, LB)

"It's Time We Had THAT Talk"

A teen-ager said, "I'm not an expert on sex. I wish my parents knew that and would tell me the things I need to know." Another teen said, "I can't talk to my parents about sex because they'd think I had a sick mind." Other teens say, "I don't think my parents would understand my views; therefore, I don't talk to them or ask them questions," or, "I've tried to ask Mom some questions but what I ask her seems to embarrass her, and she won't look at me."

Why is it so difficult to discuss sex with our teens? Do most of us feel that sex is such a private subject that there is no appropriate time or effective way to approach it? Or do we feel that even if we did tell the truth about sex our teens might not accept the whole package?

But we can't avoid talking about sex. Our teens are experiencing confusing new urges. These sensations have to find expression, release, satisfaction. Teens can't understand why they're feeling this way. In the past, boys couldn't stand to be around girls, but now the girls are beginning to look good to them. The girls also can't imagine why boys are starting to look so interesting.

Some of our teens experience guilt and shame because of these new feelings. They feel that there's no way they can face their parents with what they're experiencing. These urges can't be suppressed forever. Guilt can't go on forever. Ignorance about sex should never be allowed —but it is. Pregnant girls are resentful because their parents never told them anything about reproduction. Boys are angry because no one ever told them how they could release their sexual urges without hurting another human being. Both sexes have strong biological urges, and they don't know how to deal with them. They do know that they certainly aren't ready to accept the responsibilities that go with the urges.

Accept the fact that teens have a consuming interest in everything that is sexual. I realized this when I was teaching a group of teen-agers. I asked them to draw a circle. They were to divide the circle into wedges of varying sizes to indicate how they spent their time. Most of the wedges included such things as eating, sleeping, studying, or getting ready for school. As we discussed this, a group of boys over in one corner was laughing. The boy they were laughing at finally showed his circle. It wasn't divided into wedges. He had made a circle and had written in it, "Think about sex 100 percent." He was probably one of the most honest teens in the group.

Who's Going to Tell?

So who's going to tell them about sex? You'll probably be the most reliable source they'll have. That should make you feel so necessary and valuable that you want to do something about it. But how will you ever be able to talk with your teens about sex without embarrassing both of you? Try to look at it this way—what is your embarrassment compared to your teens' ignorance about a subject that will affect the rest of their lives?

Some of your teens may try to reassure you with, "Mom, it's okay. I know everything. I've heard all about it from my friends." You will then let them know that you, too, are available as a source of information, in case they want to check out the validity of their friends' knowledge. Let them know that even in your "sunset" years, your physical love as husband and wife is still very much an integral part of your lives and that later you want them to experience the same meaningful relationship with another person. At first it'll be difficult for them to believe that their parents can still experience that kind of an intimate relationship. It'll be equally hard for them to accept the fact that they were conceived in the same way that their friends were. However, after the initial shock, there will be a leveling-off period when they will begin to understand that there is more to learn about sex than "having sex."

If we don't feel a deep and spiritual obligation to tell our teens what they need to know and why they need to know it, we may be saying that we're going to leave their sexual education to chance, accept that they'll learn about sex in some hallway at school, or hope that someone will take the initiative to inform them. They'll find out what sex is all about whether we choose to tell them or not. They'll hear rumors that there is detailed sexual information in the encyclopedia—even pictures—and they'll start checking out the "S" volume at the school library. They'll get their hands on those six-inch-thick illustrated medical books and read parts of them again and again. They'll get in on lots of sex jokes. They'll find a secluded place to read as many torrid love stories as they can. They'll see as many movies about love and sex as they can.

Most of the things they'll be seeing, hearing, and reading will illustrate or at least suggest the sex act itself. This will reveal to them the biological side of sex (many times the attitudes will be distorted). But you know that there's more to sex than the act itself. This may be the point at which you will want to enter into your teens' lives and let them know that sex is more than a biological release.

When and How Are You Going to Tell?

One psychologist said that parents should start discussing the basics of sex with their children at ten years of age. This sounds reasonable, but what about parents who haven't yet said anything, and whose children are already teen-agers? No matter how old they are, start now!

It may be a struggle for both you and your teens, so admit to your difficulty and start at a comfortable place. There's no doubt that by the time your children become teens, they're ready to hear something on the subject, and they're hoping that you'll be the one to introduce it. Of course it would be disastrous to announce to your teens, "Each Tuesday night at seven we will meet together and talk about sex." Teens are more responsive in relaxed, impromptu situations. When they want to know something and they ask us, I believe we should give them the information within the limits of our knowledge and our own comfort. The answers we give will determine whether they will feel free to ask other questions.

When the time arrives, we should have in mind how we're going to begin talking with our teens. I don't believe any parents have the ability to tell any teen all that's involved in sexuality in one brief conversation. One mother admitted trying it this way. She didn't know if she wanted to hurry up and get it over with before embarrassment set in, or if, when she did get started, she just didn't know where to stop. With her second teen, she tried a different approach. She nonchalantly began to bring up certain facts of life, but usually, in the middle of her well-planned presentation, her daughter would say, "I already know that!" The mother, believing that her daughter actually did know everything, stopped trying to tell her anything. Later, the mother discovered that what her daughter was learning was degrading sex and that sex was becoming a frightening thing for her. During the girl's senior-high school years, she was fortunate enough to have a biology teacher who was able to help her understand the wholesomeness of sex.

Some teens' openness is an invitation for sharing the things you know and want them to know. They will usually talk when the occasion arises, as a natural outgrowth of their interest. One father decided it was time for him to start talking to his teen-aged daughters about sex. He got "his book" out, and one by one he took the girls into a room for a frank discussion. One daughter laughed, but the other one cried. The information was the same, but the results weren't. Since that beginning, this man and his wife, through the years, have been able to share their own healthy outlook on sex with their daughters.

Although it is good to be able to talk with your teens about sex, there are other ways that you can relay this knowledge to them. Many parents resort to books to help explain sex. There are probably two reasons why they depend on books. Parents may have been so influenced by Victorian teachings that it is extremely difficult for them to talk with their teens about sex. The other reason parents might recommend books is strictly as a way to help their teens gain more accurate knowledge. Either reason is acceptable and should be considered.

Some parents have access to medical books which can help them explain various aspects of sex. Still others check with librarians or bookstore managers to see what books are available and which ones give the most accurate information. Physicians are cooperative about sharing booklets with parents who want to be sure that they're telling their teens what they should know. Pastors are usually able to recommend books that deal with the Christian view of sex. Two of the most effective books I've ever read are *Between Parent and Teenager* by Dr. Haim Ginott and *The Stork Is Dead* by Charlie W. Shedd. The information in these books is precise and will never be outdated. You and your teens would benefit from both of these books. Some parents don't know how their teens will react to sex-oriented books (or do they?), so they are discreet and place the books around the house in obvious places. If teens take advantage of these books they may want to talk about some of the things they've learned from the reading. I believe that teens appreciate parents who make information available.

Encourage your teens to take part in discussions about sex that are available through churches, schools, and community programs. Your approval of their participation in these activities lets them know that you feel it's important for them to develop a healthy attitude toward their sexuality.

What Are You Going to Say?

Try to recall all of the questions you wish you had asked your parents about sex, or how you wish they had broached the subject so you wouldn't have had to be the one to ask questions. You were no different than your own teen-agers are now. Let them know how hesitant you were to ask your parents anything about sex, and that because of your hesitancy you were left in ignorance about many things. Let them know that many of the things you learned came from unreliable sources and that you became confused with your sexual development.

Tell your teens you want them to learn about sex from the right perspective and in a healthy way. Let them know that you're willing to share the knowledge that you have if they'll give you a chance. Tell them that sex isn't something that is isolated from the rest of their lives, but will affect everything they do from now on. Sex is an integral part of all our lives—teens included. If we don't help them to acknowledge, understand, value, and enjoy their sexual lives, we could be indirectly responsible for causing them unnecessary pain. So what are you going to tell them?

Girls not only need to be told about menstruation before it starts, but they also need to know why girls menstruate. Your daughters may pick up this first bit of information from other girls or from films they see at school, but the why will probably be left up to you.

One teen-ager who was having difficulty accepting the fact that she had started her menstrual period told her mother, "I wish I wasn't a woman." Her mother responded:

> Do you know why you have periods? God is preparing you to be a mother some day. Let me explain what is happening inside your body.
>
> Your body has been designed to conceive babies. Each month your uterus gets prepared for this conception. The lining grows, and by the middle of your cycle, a small egg begins to nest within your uterus. It will nest there approximately twenty-seven days. If the egg is not fertilized, there is a sudden decrease in the level of hormones in your body. The lining is then expelled and immediately a new cycle begins.
>
> Because of this sudden decrease in the level of hormones, which usually starts about forty-eight hours before you start your period, you might become irritable or depressed. When you know this might happen, you learn how to deal with moods you might have a hard time explaining.
>
> Your feminine characteristics are due to this menstrual process. Your muscle tone, soft voice, round shape, and even the texture of your hair is affected because of the menstrual process.

It is absolutely necessary that teen-age girls understand about the ovulation time. The ovulation time can be explained in this way: In the middle of the cycle the egg is released from the ovary. It travels through a tube to get to the uterus. Only one sperm from the male is required to fertilize this egg. If a couple has intercourse during ovulation, there is a very good chance that a pregnancy will occur because of the millions of sperm that the male releases. Girls must know that during their ovulation time their sex drive becomes much more intense. If they are not aware of this, they will not understand why they might easily give in to the strong drive of the male.

Teen-age boys need to know that they will begin to experience wet dreams. Many of them will not know how to cope with these dreams if they do not have this natural process explained to them. The boys need to know that the dreams aren't preplanned; they just happen, and you need to tell them why. Your explanation might follow this pattern: At this time of life the secretion of hormones becomes more intense. When this secretion is at its peak, young men become attracted to the opposite sex. Possibly they aren't attracted to any particular girl; all girls look good. During this period they start having wet dreams. They need to know that this is natural, and they should not feel guilty for having them.

Your teens will also discover masturbation (if they haven't already). This will likely be a most difficult subject for your teens to bring up. You may have a strong suspicion that they've discovered this practice, but they will usually choose to struggle through it alone. An indirect approach to this situation is through books. The books by Ginott and Shedd, as well as *Understanding Youth* (Appendix A) by Dorothy and T. Garvice Murphree, are excellent resource books to help teens understand the pros and cons of masturbation. Your teens may be relieved to read that this practice is universal and in no way suggests abnormality. I like the advice Mr. Shedd shares with teens:

> So long as masturbation is not humiliating, so long as it helps you to keep on the good side of sociable; so long as you can accept it as a natural part of growing up; then you thank God for it and use it as a blessing![1]

1. Charlie W. Shedd, *The Stork Is Dead* (Waco, TX: Word, Inc., 1976), p. 73.

This basic information will eventually help prepare our teens to start building relationships with the opposite sex. Understanding the changes their bodies are going through will help them have satisfying relationships.

Every parent of teen-age daughters always hopes that the parents of teen-age sons have explained to their boys about the boys' strong sexual drives. These young men face a society that, on the one hand, will condemn them if they misuse their urges, but, on the other, keeps giving them exaggerated ideas of what they must do, sexually, to be "a man." Parents won't have to tell their sons that they will be easily aroused—they've already confronted this new struggle. The boys can feel their urges activate by carrying on conversations about sex, having physical or eye contact with a girl, watching a girl walk down the halls at school, or noticing the way a girl dresses. Boys live in an era of exposed shoulders, midriffs, and legs, and they're getting confusing messages. These things excite them, but they must learn to control themselves.

The parents of teen-age boys are hoping that the parents of teen-age girls have told their daughters about the force of males' strong sexual drives. It is hard for some girls to understand that boys think differently about the opposite sex than they do. If the girls do not have brothers, they may not actually believe this fact until they experience it for themselves. Girls, listening to the same conversations about sex, don't react the way boys do. Most girls are totally oblivious to the structure of a boy's sexual feelings when those feelings are directed at them.

A teen-age girl said that she liked to be kissed. Then she said, "I don't understand how a boy could get 'horny' just by being kissed." Her mother asked if "horny" meant "aroused." The girl replied, "Oh! I hate that word. Can't you use a different one? Anyway, you know what I mean!" Then the mother and daughter talked about clothing. The mother emphasized how even the way a girl dresses could make a boy "horny." Her daughter said, "No one could ever get turned on by me—flat chest, big hips."

This typical conversation is evidence that many teen-age girls do not understand the strong sex drives of young men. By being aware of this fact about boys, girls can assist boys to remain in control of their emotions.

I can remember telling one of our daughters that it doesn't take a boy long to become sexually excited. However, I failed to tell her that even though it takes most girls longer to become aroused, once they are, it's extremely difficult for them to control their feelings. This is a crucial point to make to girls. They should be told not to tamper with or create such a situation, even if it sounds exciting at the time. The results are never quite as satisfying as the girls think they might be.

Girls have trouble accepting the value that a boy's peer group attaches to sex relations. She must be aware of this so that she will not allow herself to be used to satisfy a boy's desire for peer acceptance and so she won't become one more of his "conquests." Boys must be aware that the effects of loose morals are just the opposite for girls. The girls not only lose peer respect, but they also lose their self-respect.

In summary, boys must admit to their strong sexual urges and adjust to them in a healthy manner. Girls need to understand that they look at sex differently than do boys; both boys and girls must learn to respect the emotions of the opposite sex.

"I Think I'm in Love"

What's more normal for teens but more feared among us parents than for them to start dating? It isn't that we disapprove; we want them to date. But we'd like to choose whom they'll date, where they'll go on a date, and what they'll say and do on the date. We'd choose for our daughters less-experienced daters (the "skinny boy on the beach" type) and for our sons we'd choose the girls that don't quite fill out tight T-shirts. We'd have them always be in a group atmosphere and not go past holding hands on the way home.

Imagination reaches its peak during these years. We think a lot about our teens getting too serious too soon. We think about them being attracted to the wrong people. We think about all the implications of steady dating. We think about two young people out together, capable of expressing an intense love for each other.

Some of our fears come from our own dating experiences. We remember the intensity of those experiences. We remember the hurts which resulted when we were rejected by someone that we had felt loved us as much as we loved him or her. And then we had a fear of not being loved by anyone—ever. Our present fears must yield to the knowledge that out of the pains and pleasures of dating, our teens are going to learn how to relate to other human beings, just as we did. This process was established years ago when God gave man a woman. At the completion of His creation, He looked at them and everything else He had created and saw that "it was very good" (Gen. 1:31a, KJV).

Even if we admit that dating is here to stay, it's still difficult for us to see our teens with dates for the first few times. One father said that it was a traumatic experience for him when he saw a boy with his arm around his daughter. The father, who was carrying a cup of coffee at the time, spilled it all over himself. He remarked, "It was such a new experience for me, but I'm doing better now; I don't spill as much coffee." A mother saw a boy kissing her daughter and resented it. She thought, "What's he up to?" Another father said, "It's a funny feeling to see a young man who is in no way related to the family kissing my daughter."

Since these personal encounters will recur, you should try to help your teens become more comfortable around the opposite sex. I believe gradual dating experiences are the way to start. If you've told your teen, "You're not going to date until you're sixteen" (what's so magical about that number?), you're running the risk of not allowing your teens to gradually learn about the opposite sex.

Parents have to form a social league and throw their doors open to teens. I've heard many parents say, "There's no place for our kids to go on a date." But there is—the teens' homes. You say that you're willing to throw your doors open, but you don't know what to do with the young people after they've come inside? You already know that teens like to be where there is excitement. That includes eating, music, and games. As I've worked with teens, I have come to understand that body-contact games suppress teens' physical urges. Because of the national interest in recreation, numerous game books are being published. Here are two examples of body-contact games.

> Birdie on the Perch: The couples form two circles. The boys are on the outside, girls on the inside, facing each other. Blow a whistle (I use a cowbell or a duck call) to begin the boys moving clockwise and girls, counterclockwise. When the whistle is blown a second time, the girls run to their partners (who have knelt with one knee on the floor). Each girl jumps on her partner's knee and puts her arm around his neck. The last couple to assume the "birdie on the perch" position is eliminated. The game continues until only one couple is left.

> Another game calls for two nylon stockings to be tied together to make a circle. Make two such circles and divide the couples into two groups. See how many people can get inside the circles without breaking them. The group having the most bodies inside its circle is the winner.

These games go on and on. They're wild, but they have a threefold purpose: you have your teens in an active atmosphere, they're having fun with each other, and the body contact is a healthy outlet for their physical urges.

You can already see the energy, time, and planning it takes when you invite a group of teens into your home, but don't get tired yet—there's more. Games aren't the only things that make these gatherings successful. Anywhere there is a group of teens there are big appetites. If your budget doesn't allow you to feed fifteen to twenty teen-agers, ask each one of them to bring certain ingredients for banana splits, submarine sandwiches, tacos, or other refreshments. Another idea is to borrow several manual ice-cream freezers. Ask the girls to bring the ingredients for ice cream. Divide the boys into freezing teams, the girls into cheering sections, and be prepared to see a display of masculine strength which you will not see equaled during any Olympic competition as the boys see who can freeze their ice cream first.

Pairing off becomes a normal outgrowth of these group situations. The teens will find out at first that they aren't nearly as comfortable alone with each other as they are in a group. However, even during single dating, activities should be encouraged. Bowling, skating, jogging, racquetball, tennis, or any sport that requires lots of energy will quiet the sexual urges.

Eventually parents relax when they feel they've done their best and have introduced some wholesome contacts which serve as a basis for more complex relationships.

Solo Dating

Parents experience Utopia while their teens are group dating. Solo dating intrudes into this complacency. Take time to brief your teens about the implications that are going to be involved between young couples, especially those who are dating steadily.

In these briefings, we need to let our teens know that loving a particular person is not wrong, but that when the relationship begins to be anything but wholesome, it becomes wrong. Help your teens recognize that when their expressions of love go beyond a kiss and simple embrace, they may not realize the explosive situation they could be getting themselves into.

Teens are usually in control of their emotions on the

first dates with each other, but the steadier the dating, the more there will be kisses and embraces that won't be quite so simple to control. The intensity of bodily contact sets in motion a natural course of action. Many teens will tell you that they can handle any dating situation and they'll keep saying it loud and clear until the discussed situation becomes a reality. Then they'll have to make some quick decisions. The misinformed or uninformed girl may respond favorably to a boy's show of affection, and the misinformed or uninformed boy may consider the girl's response as an assent to intercourse.

Let your daughter know, before she gets too involved in steady dating, the extent of a boy's strong sex drives. Let her know that a simple gesture such as allowing a boy to caress her shoulder or touch her thigh could easily lead to much more. Your son should be informed that a girl does not usually have these strong urges. Guidelines in dating should be established before these situations begin to present themselves. Talk to your teens about deciding what they will allow to happen on a date. They should then determine to stay within those perimeters on their dates.

Teens want to be able to love as freely as they choose, but freedom carries some restrictions. Loving a person to the highest degree of physical expression is serious business. Our teens' early dating experiences and the way they react in these dating relationships will eventually culminate in a love that can be fully expressed through the act of intercourse. Every teen should have access to this quote:

> When heavy petting or intercourse is experienced outside of marriage, the fusing of two lives, in all of their experiences, moods, needs, goals, interests, and potentials is impossible. Sex becomes primarily a biological release, and while the unmarried partners might experience deep emotions, they miss the most creative potentials of sex. Later, within marriage, emotional and mental patterns

will have been set so that the greatest contribution of sex to life will be elusive.[2]

Why Sex?

One of my daughters said, "Mom, surely in this world there are some young men who don't expect you to go to bed with them at the end of every date. I don't know why it embarrasses me to say 'no.' Maybe I'm embarrassed for them because they think this is the way a date is supposed to end." I remember saying, "You'll never regret waiting." I wish I could have been a stronger supporter, but I believe she read my implication into that short statement.

Our teens can choose between two standards. The one standard has all kinds of flaws in it. It's selfish, impersonal, uncaring, uncertain, and destructive. The other standard considers whole persons: their effectiveness and their worth. Yet we hear more about the first standard. I refer to society's view regarding sex. I have come to detest this standard because it encourages our teens to believe that premarital sex is all right as long as you feel that you love each other. If you want to experience free love and have a love child, it's perfectly all right. So teens and adults do it. This standard fails, however. What society demands and what it promotes are totally contradictory. It's a double standard—teens are told to abstain from sexual activities but at the same time are bombarded by provocative advertisements and movies that are going to stimulate them sexually.

I am aware that society is a strong, ever-present force, but even with its great strength and influence, society's views have nothing to do with the real meaning of sex. Society has learned only how sex can be manipulated and misused. If you believe in the Bible, you believe that God

2. Dorothy and T. Garvice Murphree, *Understanding Youth* (Nashville: Convention Press, 1969), p. 162.

created everything. Everything that God created was good. "Everything" includes the creation of sex. Because God created it, it is sacred. According to God's standard, love between two people is sacred. It is to be dedicated; it is to be set apart to honor Him. I am sure that God foresaw the problem we have when we are faced with two standards from which to choose. He knew we could not be completely free from society's influences, so He gave us some guidelines to help us develop to our fullest potentials.

Our teens find society's guidelines attractive, while the spiritual guidelines may look as if they're dripping with old-fashioned lace. The values may seem obsolete and may carry with them a seemingly impossible amount of control and restrictions. So how do we let our teens know what's right and what's wrong? Their common sense should tell them that a thing is wrong when it hurts them and other people. Therefore, the misuse of sex is wrong. Teens need to be told what the relationship between males and females should mean. They should know what the opposite sex expects out of dating relationships, the dangers of petting, how premarital intimacies will affect their lives and their futures, the morals they will have to choose as their guidelines, the right time when they will share their lives with another person in a marriage relationship.

What do you do and what can you do so your teens have sufficient knowledge about this area of their lives? You present all the facts: biological, social, and spiritual, and then you allow them to make their own choices. But your responsibility doesn't end there. Every time they walk out the door to go on a date, you pray that God will give them the desire to use their young love for each other wisely.

The Finish Line

Those of us who have guided children all the way through the teen years have some personal experiences to share with those who still have teen-agers. First, we'd like to tell you what you don't do when your teens are ready to leave home. You don't purchase a black wreath to hang on your front door. You don't remind your teens every day how much you're going to miss them. You don't get the idea that you've outlived your usefulness.

I refuse to believe anything negative about teens leaving home. I wouldn't be honest if I didn't tell you that as the time got closer for each of our teens to leave, I wondered how I would react. I couldn't imagine how life would be without daily contact with them. Now I've experienced the exodus of our three daughters, and I can tell you unashamedly that life continues to introduce new purposes for me.

In the past years, I have had the privilege of watching three works of art in progress at the same time, each one in different stages. From the beginning of my role as a parent, I have understood intellectually that I was to love and nurture these children. With my heart, I had to understand and accept the truth that my biggest task was to prepare them to leave me. Now I can tell you why it must be this way. In their late teens our children begin to reconstruct their lives, apart from us. They have been set free, a goal that they have said they've wanted from year thirteen.

While they've been in the process of becoming independent from us, we have had a new thought forming in our minds: we must allow ourselves to become independent of them. Look at our independence like this: Now we can have chicken gizzards, liver and onions, beans and cornbread, and cooked cereal, without hearing someone comment, "Yuk" or "Gross." We can eat out more. We can buy better cuts of meat. We will save on the gas and electric bills. We might be able to get by with one car. Our schedules won't be quite as full. We'll have to do laundry only once a week. Our sleep won't be disturbed by a hair dryer or a shower going at odd hours of the night. We won't be listening for the back door to quietly open after curfew. These are some of the minor compensations of becoming independent of our teens. One of the major compensations is that our teens are going to be happy in their lives, and we're going to be happy in ours. What more could we ask?

The Last Year

A progression of detachments starts taking place during our teens' senior year of high school. It comes in a series of "lasts." It takes shape as we're typing their final last-minute research papers, or making the last trip to school to take them something they've forgotten. We begin to realize that they've taken part in their last bake sale, pep assembly, ball game, school play, concert, and debate. We've finished giving them money for their senior-class rings, caps and gowns, graduation invitations, senior trips, teachers' gifts, and overdue school bills. We don't know where the extra money came from, but somehow we've even managed to buy them the traditional graduation gift of luggage.

We get our cameras ready to take pictures of their last high-school event—graduation. We stand in their honor as they march down the aisle to the strains of "Pomp and Circumstance," noticing that no one's cap is on at the same angle. We listen to someone sing "I Shall Never Pass This Way Again." The valedictory speech is delivered; those receiving awards are recognized; diplomas are presented.

The graduation exercises are over. Classmates start hugging each other. Some of them cry. In this final moment their school loyalty is in evidence. Even though they've complained about rules, teachers, tests, and cafeteria food; even though they've been disappointed when they weren't chosen for certain honors, didn't have a date for homecoming or the prom, or didn't get to go to the state play-offs; even though they've had flare-ups with their friends and the "establishment"; all of these things are forgotten, their minds reflecting only on the twelve years of fun and security.

Our teens have become independent, although they will not be able to express what they feel at the time. The severed ties will not be completely recognized until summer is over, and these friends have scattered to begin jobs or attend college as they prepare for their futures.

Special Strokes for Special Folks

We parents aren't out of our teens' lives after the teens go to college, get a job, or get married. Now we have time (a quantity we always said we wanted) to occasionally fill their lives with unexpected surprises. Parental interest and concern don't end when teens no longer live at home.

For instance, teens away from home for the first time develop phobias about empty mailboxes. Some parents despise writing letters, but I have a cure for that. Picture your teens coming into their dorms or apartments after a tiring day, receiving a failing grade on a test, working for an indifferent employer, having a boy/girlfriend argument, or not getting the date they wanted. Then, to color their day more gray, they find nothing, not even a "To the occupant" letter, in their mailboxes. Does this make you feel guilty? I hope so.

There are several ways, other than letters, to let your teens hear from you. Send tape-recorded messages from the family. Write a week's supply of encouraging Scriptures on separate cards. Tell your teens to take one card from the envelope each day and meditate on its promise before they begin each busy day. Write letters in the form of prayers, specifically mentioning your teens in prayer —prayers of thanksgiving for their lives, prayers of supplication asking God to make His presence known to them as they make decisions, as they study or work, and as they relate to other people.

When they've received a special honor, had a part in a play, performed in a concert, or done well in a particular sport, send them a telegram to share in their happiness. If their birthdays fall during the school year, ask family members, including grandparents and favorite aunts and uncles, to surprise your teens with card showers. Contact your teens' friends and ask them to organize a singing telegram for the birthday. Or what could be more special than wiring your teens flowers or a potted plant—for no reason at all—with a note bearing the message, "We love you"?

If you don't live close enough to send "Care" packages to your teens, conspire with their roommates or other friends to help you carry out your plans. Send these friends some money and ask them to fix a box filled with fruits, cookies, cheeses, soups, juices, teabags, and gum (not necessarily all at one time). According to the season, ask them to add other items to the box: a small pumpkin, a Thanksgiving or a Christmas item that can be displayed in their rooms, a box of Valentine candy, an inexpensive stuffed rabbit. Know when your teens are studying for mid-term or final exams. While they're eating the food that you've provided, they'll be remembering their family and how you're backing them during these special times.

One of the best ways to be a popular parent is to take homemade food items when you visit your teens. Any flavor, size, shape, or color of cake or cookies is well-received. It's fun to see how many of the other teens automatically nickname you "Mom" and "Dad" because you've personalized your visit by bringing something to share with them. Taking your teens and their friends out to eat in a restaurant or on a picnic at least once during your visit will warrant a thank-you note from them after you've returned home.

When your teens come home for a visit, do your best to make it a special time for them. When our daughters come home, I literally roll out a red carpet for them. It's fifteen feet of evidence that I love them, that I'm glad they've come home, and that for a brief time, I am privileged to enjoy their company.

None of us ever know the complete effect that our prayers have upon our teens when they're away from home. They don't share many of the things they're going through, but we automatically know that they will always need the extra spiritual strength that comes through prayer. During those times when we can't reach out and touch our teens, hear their voices, see them, or know what they're experiencing, we can pray.

God, I pray for our children today. I offer them up to you. When I do this I can go about my work, knowing that you have enclosed their lives in your safekeeping. I am asking that you give them the physical, mental, and spiritual strengths they will need today. Thank you, Lord, for their lives. Amen.

Let's Be Friends

One day I was taking a walk with one of our older daughters. We started talking about our relationship with each other. My daughter said, "Mom, you've meant many different things to me through the years, but now I think of you as my friend." I wanted to stop right there and give her a hug, but I contained myself and agreed that I felt the same way about her. I have enjoyed special friendships all my life, but never has a statement sounded more beautiful than when my daughter said she is my friend. I have had similar experiences with my other two daughters, and we now have become equals. Our experiences since we have been apart have been different, yet we remain equals in our basic beliefs. Even though I have had more years of living than they have, this has not kept us from being able to relate to each other. Our teens' independence from my husband and me forced them to come to terms with the adult world, and they have returned to us in a new relationship. The greatest compliment children can give to their parents is to be able to function successfully in the adult world.

I have stated in other parts of this book that our teens' having become independent of us doesn't mean that they've stopped loving us. Our relationship is different now. We now have a love that accepts and respects the worth of each person.

. . . A Little Later

I baked chocolate chip cookies a week ago, but I have this problem—there are still some left. The potato chips I thought my husband and I could eat are stale. I have to keep reminding myself to put the bread in the refrigerator so that it won't become moldy before we can eat it. I must remind myself to set only two plates for our meals. The stereo, radio, and television are off. The house is quiet. Is this the tranquil scene that kept flashing before my eyes during those busy years with our teens when I felt I had to be alone?

Now I have time to reflect, to evaluate, to summarize, to finalize. And now the questions come. "Why didn't I . . .?" "Was it wrong to . . .?" "If we had . . . would they have . . .?" "How could we have . . .?" "Have we been able to . . .?" "Do you think they'll remember . . .?" My questions are answered when I remember a letter that came from our oldest daughter:

Mom and Dad:

I've been thinking about the kind of life I've had with you. We've all had our growth periods. Some of them have been painful, but I think we've had a terrific, even rare, relationship with each other. I have no regrets about my upbringing, none—you're the best!

Parental mission accomplished!

Bibliography

Ginott, Haim G. *Between Parent and Teenager.* New York: Macmillan, 1969; paperback edition, New York: Avon Books, 1973.
Dr. Ginott shows parents how they can open new lines of communication with their teens. As the father of teen-age children, he discusses the subjects from both a parental and professional point of view.

Murphree, Dorothy and T. Garvice. *Understanding Youth.* Nashville: Convention Press, 1969.
The authors discuss youth and sexuality in Appendix A. They approach the subject of sex from the Christian viewpoint, and also consider the "why?" of sex.

Satir, Virginia. *Peoplemaking.* Palo Alto, CA: Science and Behavior Books, Inc., 1972.
This family therapist's main goal is not only to tell families how important communication is, but also to explain how they can successfully communicate.

Shedd, Charlie W. *The Stork Is Dead.* Waco, TX: Word, Inc., 1976.
The author has tremendous insight about the teen-age years, because he is a father of teens. His book offers "plain talk" about every subject that is related to teens.